Where in the World?

Published by
The Bible Reading Fellowship
15 The Chambers, Vineyard
Abingdon OX14 3FE
United Kingdom
Tel: +44 (0)1865 319700
Email: enquiries@brf.org.uk
Website: www.brf.org.uk
BRF is a Registered Charity

ISBN 978 0 85746 155 1

First published 2012
10 9 8 7 6 5 4 3 2 1 0

Acknowledgments
Unless otherwise stated, scripture quotations are taken from the Contemporary English Version of the Bible, HarperCollins Publishers, copyright © 1991, 1992, 1995 American Bible Society.

Scripture taken from the Holy Bible, New International Reader's Version®. Copyright © 1996, 1998 Biblica. All rights reserved throughout the world. Used by permission of Biblica.

p. 18: Corrymeela prayer reprinted by kind permission of the Corrymeela Community, Northern Ireland.

p. 21: Arabic song *Laylatal Milad* ('On the eve of Christmas') by Fr Mansour Lebeke, translated by Rev Dr Naim Ateek, reprinted by kind permission of Sabeel Ecumenical Liberation Theology Center, Jerusalem.

p. 72: Prayer from China, from *Lilies of the Field*, Janice and Philip Wickeri (ed., trans.) (The Foundation for Theological Education in Southeast Asia). Reprinted by kind permission of the publisher.

Every effort has been made to trace and contact copyright owners for material used in this book. We apologise for any inadvertent omissions or errors, and would ask those concerned to contact us so that full acknowledgment can be made in the future.

The paper used in the production of this publication was supplied by mills that source their raw materials from sustainably managed forests. Soy-based inks were used in its printing and the laminate film is biodegradable.

A catalogue record for this book is available from the British Library

Printed in the UK by MWL.

Where in the World?

An RE and assembly resource on
the worldwide Christian Church

Martyn Payne

Photocopy permission

The Copyright Licensing Agency (CLA)

BRF is a Registered Charity (No. 233280)

Contents

Foreword

Watching swallows swooping over Rwandan skies, with the mountains behind, is a wonderful sight. Then to remember that these same birds may, at another point in the year, be flying above my home in Southwell is quite awe-inspiring. The same world, the same bird, and the same church and Christian faith, which see me in both places. Yet the way this faith is expressed and lived out is different—because of our different histories, cultures, climates, economies, language and so much more.

It is my huge privilege to have experienced the church in many different parts of the world. It is wonderfully diverse and rich, with such a wealth of ways of worship and prayer, of teaching and learning, of engaging with the needs of communities and nations. The church is dynamic because the Christian faith is dynamic. The church is found in every nation on earth, sometimes in very small numbers, sometimes in very large numbers. It is found expressing itself in a host of traditions and styles: simply to use Orthodox, Catholic, Protestant and Pentecostal as broad brush-strokes for the four main movements is to hide a huge variety within each of these traditions, and to fail to notice the interweaving between them.

If we want children to have anything like a basic understanding of Christianity, they need *both* the core central beliefs common to all Christian traditions (of God as Creator, loving the world; of Jesus Christ, his life, teaching, death, resurrection, ascension and future hope; of the Holy Spirit; of humanity and all creatures made and loved by God, and of the church) *and* to know that it is a worldwide faith, rich in its life of worship, prayer, witness and engagement.

This book by Martyn Payne, who knows so much of this wealth, is a wonderful resource to help children into this rich, rich world of the global church. It deserves to be very widely used by schools of all kinds, for it will not only help children to understand the church and the Christian faith more fully; it will also simply help them to understand our amazingly diverse world, bound in its common humanity, more fully.

Enjoy. Use. Be enriched.

The Rt Revd Paul Butler
Bishop of Southwell and Nottingham

Introduction

> 'People will come from east and west and north and south. They will take their places at the feast in God's kingdom.'
>
> LUKE 13:29 (NIRV)

Bigger than you think!

The Christian Church is bigger than you think! Over the 2000 years since Jesus chose his small band of **disciples** in the Roman province of Judea, it has grown into a family of over two billion believers, who today can be found in every country of the world.

The low points

The story of how the Christian faith spread across the globe is a remarkable one, full of many twists and turns that involved bravery and foolishness, sacrifice and insensitivity, and individual heroism alongside, sadly, much misdirected zeal and prejudice. Many people today, looking at the history of Christianity, are rightly upset and saddened by the many stains on its 2000-year history. Terrible religious wars or examples of cruel judgmental attitudes towards others are indeed things of which Christians should be deeply ashamed, and all the more so because these attitudes stand in contrast to the message of peace, reconciliation and forgiveness that Jesus Christ lived and preached. It seems that matters of belief, which are so fundamental to how we human beings choose to live our lives, can easily become a source of pride and a cause of division rather than unity.

The high points

Fortunately, this is not the whole story. The inner transformation that Christians experience through putting their trust in Jesus Christ as God has also led to radical changes in society for good. Many schools, hospitals, charities and relief agencies trace their origins to the hard work of people of faith, who wanted to love their neighbour as themselves and recognised that every human life is precious to God. These people were inspired by God's love for them to make a difference, by challenging injustices, relieving suffering and helping to mend this broken world—in short, to establish the kingdom of God, about which Jesus had spoken.

Going global

Today, groups of Christian believers can be found meeting for worship across the world in many different types of churches, from ornate cathedrals to tin tabernacles; and in a wide variety of locations, from megacities such as Seoul in South Korea to villages on the slopes of Mount Kilamanjaro in Tanzania; and among all manner of ethnic groups and cultures, from the nomadic tribesmen of Mongolia to Sudanese refugees in Egypt. Among each people group, its message has been received, interpreted and inculturated. Clearly no single expression of this dynamic faith is enough to say everything about the person and work of Jesus, and that is why each manifestation of global Christianity is needed.

Community and unity

The church on the corner within your own community is only part of a huge world jigsaw of Christianity that is still active and growing in the 21st century. Whenever teachers take a class to visit a local place of Christian worship, it is important to remember this. The building they explore is only one example of a sheltering place for 'God's everywhere people', who have developed ways to respond to the story of Jesus from within their own cultures and use local songs, prayers, symbols and stories that best help them unpack who God is and what God calls them to do.

Sharing a common focus, the person of Jesus Christ as the way into the mystery of God, every **congregation** across the world has something to offer their sisters and brothers in this world family of faith. New opportunities for travel and advances in communication technology have meant that this cross-cultural sharing is accessible to more of us. When it comes to teaching children what Christians believe and helping them explore for themselves what the faith means, a global dimension is vital to their understanding and evaluation of what Christianity is all about. I hope that this handbook will equip teachers for just this task.

Overview of the book

The material in this book has been put together to help schools meet the expectations of locally agreed RE syllabi in relation to teaching Christianity as a world-wide faith. The SIAS (Statutory Inspection of Anglican Schools) guidance document (2005), for example, puts as one of the aims of RE that 'pupils should experience the breadth and variety of the Christian community'.

The potential scope of this handbook is vast. People have written volumes about the history of the growth of the Church during the last two millennia and there continue to be new and exciting stories of the contemporary Church from all parts of the globe. There are, in addition, many different strands of Christianity, with huge variations in their approach to worship and liturgy. Theological interpretations still separate some **denominations** from each other and make shared communion difficult, and radically different interpretations of the Bible can cause heated controversy.

With so much that could be shared, there is always the danger of falling into superficiality and of presenting unfair stereotypes when opening windows into the worldwide Church. Every possible effort has been made to avoid this danger, while recognising that teachers will not want to overburden lesson material with too many caveats and footnotes. The book is intended as a broad outline to draw on, which will enhance the teacher's own knowledge and provide a wider canvas of perspective and interest for the topic that children will enjoy exploring.

To this end, it offers:

- A five-session scheme of work for the classroom.
- Information about churches in other countries.
- Material for collective worship.
- Stories for the classroom.
- Resources for exploring Christian festivals from a non-Western perspective.
- Biographies of Christian 'heroes' from other parts of the world.
- Ideas for project work.
- Links to a selection of simple Christian songs.
- Prayers from around the globe.
- Guidelines for making ethical and workable links with schools overseas.
- Links to other relevant resources and websites.
- A short glossary. (Definitions of words emboldened in the text can be found on pages 85–86.)

I hope that the stories, ideas and resources in this book will enrich your RE planning, particularly for children who are living in today's multicultural British society.

MARTYN PAYNE

Go to the website www.barnabasinschools.org.uk/whereintheworld/ to find downloadable pictures of the churches in Sparkle's story and of the global Christians in Chapter 8, together with further links and ideas to support this theme.

A five-week scheme of work for the classroom

Week 1

- **Learning objective:** To consider the question 'Where are the Christians?' and begin to understand that they are a worldwide family.

- **Introduction:** Using an interactive map, pictures from the BRF website material and a toy swallow, tell the story of Sparkle's migration from the United Kingdom to South Africa.

- **Main activity:** After talking about the story (which part of the journey did they like the best, which part surprised them, which part puzzled them, which part is most like home and which part would they rather have left out), hand out pictures of the different churches and Christian gatherings and in groups compare and contrast two pictures. Discuss what questions they would like to ask the people in the picture and what those in the picture might like to ask the class.

- **Main teaching point:** An investigation into what is a typical Christian or a typical Christian church; an exploration of what is the same and what is different compared to churches in the UK. A 'typical' Christian in the 21st century is between 20 and 30 years old, black-skinned and poor, lives in the majority world and is out of work: a Christian profile in the UK is very different.

- **Plenary activity:** Read the story of what happened at Pentecost from Acts 2—the beginning of the worldwide church—and use one of the activities in Chapter 2 to explore this story. All Bible references can be looked up at www.biblegateway.com.

Week 2

- **Learning objective:** To compare and contrast Christian worship in the United Kingdom with that in other parts of the world.

- **Introduction:** Recap the story of the swallow and the places Sparkle visited. What did the children learn about the Christian faith from the last session? What might they expect to find happening in a church service in the UK?

- **Main activity:** Using pictures, activity ideas and information from the book and the web support material, explore in groups different aspects of a church service through the eyes of the world church. Include the call to worship, baptism, Communion, prayer and sharing the Peace. Encourage the groups to come up with something that surprises them in what they discover and something that puzzles them.

- **Main teaching point:** Christianity has taken root within people groups from many cultures, and each country uses things that are familiar and meaningful to them to worship God. For example, it would be odd to describe Jesus as 'the bread of life' in a part of the world where rice is the staple food. What unites this world faith is not the ways it is expressed but the fact that there is a shared belief in Jesus as God and that Christians believe Jesus is still with them today (see 1 Corinthians 12:3 and 15:16–20a).

- **Plenary activity:** Learn a song from another part of the worldwide Christian Church. There are suggested songs in this book.

Week 3

- **Learning objective:** To explore the variety of ways in which major Christian festivals are celebrated around the world and how they give differing but complementary insights into what Christians believe.

- **Introduction:** Ask the class which they think are the main Christian festivals in the year. Perhaps some clues will help, such as a picture of a baby, a present, a donkey, a cross, a basket of fruit and a thank-you card. Christians all around the world celebrate Advent and Christmas, Lent and Easter, and Harvest. How are these festivals celebrated in the UK?

- **Main activity**: Using the information in the book and the support resources on the web, set the class off in groups to investigate how Christians in other countries celebrate these special festivals. They should look out for what is similar and what is different from celebrations in the UK. What new ideas about Jesus and God come from their research? This book also gives links to global artwork for the festivals, which would provide another way into this activity. Groups can come up with a spoken or written report on what new things they have discovered about Christmas, Easter or Harvest.

- **Main teaching point**: The shape, emphasis and focus of key Christian festivals will vary depending on where in the world the Christian community is located. Churches in poorer, rural societies might more readily identify with the humble beginnings of Jesus, born in a stable, or the importance of a good harvest where the climate is very unpredictable. Similarly, the innocent suffering of Jesus can have a greater depth of meaning where Christians are under pressure to give up their faith or where they are facing injustice. This is often reflected in the prayers they write or the art or type of cross they create. What special understandings of the Christian story can each part of the worldwide Church bring, including the church in the UK?

- **Plenary activity**: Explore the Christian image of a human body with many parts as a simile for the Christian family around the world (1 Corinthians 12:12–27). What does this picture teach us about appreciating difference and diversity? What other images can children come up with? The class could now choose to focus on one of the Christian festivals they have explored (depending on the term when this work is covered) to prepare a class assembly to present to the whole school about what they have discovered concerning Christmas, Easter or Harvest around the world.

Week 4

- **Learning objective**: To evaluate and learn from the lives of Christians around the world (historical and contemporary) and how they have lived out their faith within their own communities and beyond.

- **Introduction**: Read with the children the final words that Jesus spoke to his followers in Matthew 28:18–20 and Acts 1:8. Christianity was always meant to be an active faith that changed people and the ways of the world for the better. Jesus once told a story about a mustard seed that, though very tiny, grew to become the biggest of trees, providing shelter for the very birds that might once have eaten that seed (Matthew 13:31–32). But how has this Christian family grown so big?

- **Main activity**: In Chapter 8 there are short stories of individuals who were inspired by their Christian faith to make a difference for good in the world. Introduce a selection of these stories and ask the children to research further into who these people were, what they did, why they did it and what good things have come because of their Christian faith. Their research could be recorded as a newspaper report or a storyboard of the subject's life, or it could be turned into a small play with a series of freeze-frames, which could be digitally photographed and then have captions added. Invite groups to share with the whole class what they have found. What do they find inspirational about these stories? What might these people be doing if they were alive today or lived in your community? What difference does faith make to the way a person lives his or her life?

- **Main teaching point**: The story of the Christian faith is the story of people responding to God's love towards them and wanting to pass it on in some positive way. The church isn't a building but the people of God on the move. So many institutions, charities and educational bodies—alongside advances in science, medicine and the arts—have been begun by women and men of faith. Christians all over the world are still involved in challenging injustice, bringing healing, improving education, making peace and changing lives.

- **Plenary activity**: This is an opportunity to find out, from a partner school in the majority world, what issues the Christian church in another part of the world is facing, and to explore what the challenges might be for the Christian church in this part of the world. How might each help the other? For example, what sort of 'shoebox of gifts' might the children send and what sort of 'shoebox of help' might the children like to receive?

There are guidance notes about school twinning in the majority world in Chapter 9, as well as a folk tale to share to open up discussion.

Week 5

- **Learning objective:** To review what has been learned over this unit of work and how it might continue to influence the children's lives and the ethos of the school.

- **Introduction:** Use the swallow's return from South Africa in the spring as a vehicle to explore what the children might bring home with them from this journey around part of the worldwide Christian Church. Retrace the swallow's journey with a map, some songs (using ethnic instruments, if possible) and examples of worship and stories that the children have found in the course of this scheme of work.

- **Main activity:** Prompted by an evaluation sheet that is divided in sections to mirror the stages of the swallow's journey and the countries it has visited, ask the children to work in pairs and decide on what souvenirs they will bring 'home'. These could take the form of stories, pictures, artefacts, insights, songs, prayers, festival information or memories of the best bits for them. Which part of the journey has inspired them the most? About which part do they want to find out more? What might the children decide to do either individually or as a class, as a result of what they have learned? What new aspects of the Christian faith have they discovered?

- **Main teaching point:** Christians believe that they are called to work with God to help mend a broken world. They believe that Jesus, by his life, death and **resurrection**, has shown the way and makes a new beginning possible for everybody. The story of Jesus is still being told, and today the Christian Church is growing fastest in Africa and South America. There are, for example, more Christians in the Anglican Church of Nigeria than in the equivalent denomination in all of Western Europe. The Church is bigger than most people think, and it is growing.

- **Plenary activity:** Draw this unit to a close by inviting the children as a class to put together a short service of Christian worship, using some of their favourite discoveries from the worldwide Church from these last weeks. For example, they might use a call to prayer on the drum from Uganda, a song from Peru, a way of sharing the Peace from Romania, a picture of a Bible story from China, a verse from that same story in a language other than English, a prayer from Australia and a blessing from India.

For each week of the lesson plans above, there are further suggestions of differentiated activities for Foundation and Key Stages 1 and 2 within the chapters of this book.

You will also find lists of key questions, learning objectives, learning outcomes and learning experiences for RE, PSHE and Global Citizenship, in Appendix 3 (pages 77–80).

As a supplementary idea for learning outside the classroom, depending on where your school is located, you may be able to arrange a class visit to a church that has links with another part of the world. These groups sometimes share the use of existing local church centres—for example, a Tamil-speaking church from Sri Lanka, a black-majority church from Nigeria, a Punjabi-speaking church from Pakistan or a Filippino church. Alternatively, you might be able to arrange for a member of that church community to visit your school.

Chapter 1

Everywhere a home

Overview of content

This chapter offers a journey story to use over a series of assemblies or in the classroom as a way to begin exploring the Christian faith through the eyes of the worldwide Church. The story is based on the migration of a swallow and introduces children to a variety of churches on different continents.

Background note on the story

The migration of a swallow is one of nature's marvels. The swallows that nest in the eaves of buildings in Britain during the spring have made their way there from the other side of the world. Once their young are hatched and have learned to fly during our summer months, they set off on their 12,000 mile journey back to South Africa, where they spend the winter, wisely avoiding the cold and dark days of the northern hemisphere. British swallows migrate due south down the western side of Africa, while their European cousins take a route further to the east.

For the purposes of the following story, the swallow gets blown off course and joins his cousins, not rejoining his British family until the end.

For more on swallow migration go to: www.rspb.org.uk/wildlife/birdguide/name/s/swallow/migration.aspx

This story was inspired by verses from the Bible:

Lord God All-Powerful, your temple is so lovely! Deep in my heart I long for your temple, and with all that I am I sing joyful songs to you. Lord God All-Powerful, my King and my God, sparrows find a home near your altars; swallows build nests there to raise their young. You bless everyone who lives in your house, and they sing your praises. (Psalm 84:1–4)

Making it come alive

The story is best told with a visual of a swallow. This could be either a picture from the internet, perhaps projected on to a screen, or a soft toy swallow. The RSPB have toy swallows for sale, which also produce bird song: http://shopping.rspb.org.uk/p/SingingBirds/Swallow_singing_bird.htm

Go to the website www.barnabasinschools.org.uk/whereintheworld/ to find downloadable pictures of the churches that Sparkle visits. A shorter version of the story, to use with Foundation and Key Stage 1 (P1–3), is available on the same website.

A map of the world would also be useful, on which you could track the swallow's progress.

Story: Everywhere a home

'If you're looking for a safe place to perch, always choose the roof,' sang Sparkle's mother as they flew home one day. 'And when it comes to roofs, there is nowhere safer than the roof of a church.'

As she said this, they swooped in low over their church, back to the home where Sparkle had been born—the nest beneath the roof, from which he could hear the singing of the choir, the peal of the bells and the laughter of children.

*****

'But why must we leave all this?' moaned Sparkle.

The nest at the church had been his whole world until then. News that they must all soon fly off to another country far away had come as a real shock.

'The leaves are turning brown and the days are getting shorter,' explained his mother. 'We must find a warmer place for winter. The journey is calling us.'

'But do I really have to say goodbye to all of this?' thought Sparkle sadly.

*****

A few days later, Sparkle and his family joined a great flock, which soared and swooped its way across the countryside. His church was soon out of sight, and with it, thought Sparkle, was everything safe and familiar: the singing of the choir, the peal of the bells and the laughter of children. It was hard saying goodbye but there was no time for tears. The journey was calling them.

*****

Over fields and homes, high above rivers and hills, they flew on, following an invisible highway in the sky, until they came to their first resting place. It was the bells that most surprised and pleased Sparkle. They had settled on the roof of a grand church in the middle of a town. It was a little like home, thought Sparkle, as he watched the people arriving and heard the sounds of singing. There was even children's laughter to reassure him that all was well.

'There are other safe places, after all,' he thought. But the journey was calling them. Next day, they were up in the air, travelling south and saying goodbye again.

*****

'Help! What's happened to the land?' screeched Sparkle, as suddenly the ground below turned to shimmering blue with splashes of white.

'We're over the sea,' laughed his mother, 'and we're in luck. We can fly with a following wind.'

The flock made good time and soon reached the shores of a new country. But the wind that had helped them now turned against them. Sparkle shuddered as he felt the first huge drops of thunder-rain on his wings. The sky became dark with thick clouds and the flock dived for shelter.

*****

'Where do we go?' called out Sparkle, but the storm drowned his words. Everyone had scattered and there was no reply. Sparkle was suddenly alone and off course, buffeted by the rain and the gale. He lost sight of everyone and completely lost his sense of direction.

'Where are you? Which way do I go?' he called, but his voice could not be heard above the storm. However, something deep inside urged him forward as he longed for the safety of his little church and the sound of singing, the peal of bells and the laughter of children. The journey was calling him on.

*****

Sparkle flew blindly, riding the storm, until out of the gloom and mist he spotted forests below him. But where were the others? Where was his family? Had he lost them for ever?

The landscape was strange and frightening. There seemed to be no place to settle and rest—but then he heard it. A single bell rang out a faint welcome. He swooped down towards a small clearing on a hillside. He spotted an old wooden building covered with beautiful carvings. It was a welcome sight after the storm and the loneliness—and, in a strange way, it felt familiar.

*****

So Sparkle was not really surprised when he heard the rich sound of singing coming from inside the building. The songs weren't quite the same as the songs he'd been used to, but they did make him feel at home. This was a church, too, and a safe place. Nearby he spotted other swallows. They weren't part of his flock but they were also flying south, so perhaps there was still a chance he could meet up with his family.

Soon the journey was calling them. After only a few days, he was on the wing again, saying goodbye. The last sound he heard was the laughter of children.

*****

For days and days, Sparkle and his new companions flew on, sometimes with the wind, sometimes against it. Sparkle's wings ached with the effort. The countryside below them now was less green and more like a patchwork of greys and browns. He also noticed that the air was growing warmer.

'Look!' cried Sparkle to the others. 'What a beautiful sight.' Below them, a wide expanse of water caught the light of the setting sun. A large lake nestled between low hills and was bordered by flat-roofed houses.

*****

'We must rest again,' called the others as the flock began to circle its way down towards the land and a tall white building near the centre of a town. There were lots of places to perch among the columns and statues that decorated its walls. Near the entrance, Sparkle could see long lines of people filing into the building. There must be something very special about this place. Singing and the nearby laughter of children meant he felt safe again.

'It's where he grew up,' commented one friendly swallow. Sparkle looked puzzled.

'He's the one they're all singing about,' she explained. But before Sparkle could ask any more questions, it was already time to think about moving on. The journey was calling. Soon they were high above the church, travelling south and saying goodbye once again.

*****

Their flight this time took them across great empty plains and bare mountains. Only occasionally did small clumps of tall trees break the monotony of sand and rock. Sparkle began to feel nervous and worried. Would they ever make it to the end of the journey? Would he see his family again? He wished he were back at one of the safe places he had discovered on the way. Most of all, he longed for his church and his warm home under the roof. What would happen if they had to land in this terrible place?

*****

In the distance, smoke from a fire signposted a small cluster of huts near some trees. The flock descended to find rest, and Sparkle found himself perched upon one of the strangest buildings he'd ever seen. It was like a hill of straw and branches, with a mud wall beneath. Then, to his amazement, Sparkle heard the laughter of children from inside and watched as people streamed out, clapping and singing at the top of their voices. He could hardly believe his eyes and ears. This too was a church! They were singing about the same special person, just as the others had told him.

'Who would have guessed we would find a safe place in all this emptiness?' sang Sparkle to himself out loud. But he did not have long to enjoy the scene. The journey called them on. Sparkle took off and followed the others, travelling south and saying goodbye once again.

*****

Dusty red roads crisscrossed their way through dark green plantations in the countryside below. The rising warm air gave new energy to support tired wings. Sparkle trusted the flock to lead the way, and by now he was beginning to realise that his church was not the only one. The safety of the singing and the laughter and the peal of the bells could be found in many places.

He was so caught up in thinking about all this that he almost missed the sudden dive made by the flock as it once again made for rest and shelter.

*****

This church was different again. In some ways it seemed only half-finished, but that didn't bother the people inside. They too were singing and some even danced. Children swayed and clapped as the warm air was filled with their joy. It was so exciting that Sparkle found it hard to settle and instead joined in, diving in and out among the singers through the holes in the walls where the windows should have been.

The next day, Sparkle thought he could still hear the beat of the drums and the laughter of the children as the swallows once more prepared to leave. The journey was calling them on and soon they were travelling south, saying goodbye once again.

*****

As they flew, Sparkle learned from the others that they were all heading for the flat mountain at the end of the world. It was a warm place where they could spend the winter safely.

'Do all swallows find their way there?' asked Sparkle anxiously. 'Of course,' replied his new friends. 'Your family will be there too, but it might not be easy to find them among so many.'

Sparkle thought back over his journey so far and all the safe places he had visited. It filled his heart with hope. That night, he was sure he heard yet more singing and laughter, and even the sound of bells from a small village church near the reed bed where they settled.

*****

'Just one more day to go,' chorused the flock as they regained energy and enthusiasm for the last leg. As he swooped low over grassy plains filled with strange new animals and flew among exotic and beautiful birds he'd never seen before, the journey called Sparkle ever onward towards the flat mountain at the end of the world.

As the mountain grew closer, the air became busy with more and more swallows. Flocks joined together, weaving in and out of each other in a most amazing display of acrobatics. The sky was dense with shifting clouds of blue and red flashes as Sparkle and his many, many friends reached their journey's end. Would this be a safe place? Was this a home? Would he find his family again?

*****

It was the laughter that first caught his attention—and then children singing a special song. He turned and flew in their direction. Soon he spotted a colourful choir, processing into a building made of metal. He flew closer.

'It's one of the safe places,' thought Sparkle. He made for the roof as bells began to peal. It was almost as if they were welcoming him to his new home from home.

'I hoped you would find your way here,' called out a familiar voice. It was his mother, of course! The whole family were there. 'The storm must have blown you off course, but the journey called you on.'

'And guess what, Mum?' added Sparkle. 'Everywhere I went, I found a home!'

Chapter 2

Everywhere on the journey

Overview of content

Following on from the story, this chapter provides supporting material for each of the countries visited, with background about the Christian faith of its people, some questions and discussion starters, a few short prayers and a simple song from that region. The material can be used in conjunction with an assembly series on this theme or to enhance work in the classroom.

In Britain

A bird's-eye view of the church in Britain

This church could be your own local church. There may even be swallows nesting nearby.

Christianity probably came to Britain with the Romans in the first centuries after Christ. Further missions from both the Celtic Christian church in Ireland and the church in Rome helped to establish the Christian faith in these islands.

In the 16th century, the church in England broke its links with Rome and the Anglican Church was established. From this time, many other denominations were set up and went their own ways, choosing independence from the state church and having their own interpretations of the Bible and key Christian **doctrines**.

Many Christian mission societies began life in the UK. The Anglican and Methodist Churches, in particular, have large numbers of members beyond these shores.

Until the second half of the last century, most people had links with a church, but, in more recent years, church attendance has declined, particularly as the Western world has become more affluent. Nevertheless, one-third of Church of England churches today are growing again.

The fastest-growing denomination in the UK is Pentecostalism, with its emphasis on a lively experience of God the Holy Spirit and greater freedom in worship.

For further information, go to:
www.churchofengland.org
www.churchinwales.org.uk
www.churchofscotland.org.uk
www.ireland.anglican.org

Questions and discussion starters

- Have you ever been inside a Christian church? What were your first impressions?
- How old is the Christian church nearest to your school?
- How many people worship there?
- What sort of services does it have?
- Why do you think fewer people choose to go to church nowadays?
- How would you make the church a more welcoming place?
- What do you think is the most important thing that happens in a church?
- If you could design a new church, what would it look like?

A simple song

The song 'God is so good' (*Junior Praise* No 53) celebrates what Christians believe about God and is easy to learn.

God is so good
God is so good
God is so good
He's so good to me

Use these simple actions to accompany the words:

- God: both hands with extended index fingers pointing upwards
- Good: thumbs up on both hands
- To me: point back to yourself with both hands

Prayers

God our Father, we come to you as children.
Be with us as we learn to see one another with new eyes, hear one another with new hearts and treat one another in a new way.

A PRAYER OF THE CORRYMEELA PEACE COMMUNITY, FROM NORTHERN IRELAND

Alone with none but thee, my God
I journey on my way.
What need I fear when thou art near
O King of night and day?
More safe am I within thy hand
Than if an host didst round me stand.

ST COLUMBA

Praise be to thee, O Lord Jesus Christ, for all the benefits which thou hast given me, for all the pains and insults which thou hast borne for me. O most merciful Redeemer, friend and brother, may I know thee more clearly, love thee more dearly, and follow thee more nearly, day by day.

PRAYER OF ST RICHARD OF CHICHESTER

I bind unto myself today
the strong Name of the Trinity,
by invocation of the same
the Three in One and One in Three...
I bind unto myself today
the power of God to hold and lead,
his eye to watch, his might to stay,
his ear to hearken to my need.
The wisdom of my God to teach,
his hand to guide, his shield to ward;
the word of God to give me speech,
his heavenly host to be my guard.

PRAYER OF ST PATRICK FROM WALES, WHO WORKED AS A MISSIONARY IN IRELAND

In Austria

A bird's-eye view of the church in Europe

The story of Jesus was first preached in Europe when the **apostle** Paul was called by a vision to cross over from the Roman province of Asia Minor (modern-day Turkey) into Greece (see Acts 16:9–10).

Both the apostles Paul and Peter ended up in Rome within 30 years of the death of Jesus, and a Christian community was established there, initially as a persecuted **sect**.

A few centuries later, the Christian faith was adopted by the emperor himself and became the official religion of the Roman empire. This meant it could flourish in all parts of Europe, and it continued to survive even when the empire collapsed.

Brave missionaries, some from Britain like Boniface, took the faith to the northern European tribes. Once the king or tribal chief had been converted, the whole community began to follow the Christian way.

In the Middle Ages, the church in Europe began to split up over doctrine and practice. Much of northern Europe became **Protestant**, following the teachings of Luther and others, while, in the south, allegiance was still given to the Pope in Rome. This **Catholic** tradition remains the predominant version of Christianity here to this day.

Although large numbers still register themselves as Christian, church attendance is very low. Europe, including Great Britain, is often described as being 'post-Christian', although this has meant that those who do still follow their faith are often stronger in their commitment and evangelism.

Europe has produced a wealth of artwork based on the Christian story, particularly during the Renaissance (14th–17th centuries), as well as music and literature that has had a profound influence all over the world.

For further information, go to:
http://europe.anglican.org/homepage
www.catholic-hierarchy.org/country/at.html

Questions and discussion starters

- Is there a church of the Catholic tradition near your school?
- In what ways does Catholic worship differ from that in churches of other traditions? (Maybe you can invite a local Catholic to talk with your class or in an assembly.)
- Catholic churches tend to give greater prominence to the person of Mary, the mother of Jesus. What do you think about this? Can you find some pictures of her?
- Has anyone visited churches when they were on holiday in Europe? What was your impression of these churches?
- What do you think are the reasons people go to church?
- Why do you think some churches are more decorative than others, with artwork, sculptures and paintings?
- What is it in a church building that would most help you to pray and come close to God?

A simple song

Here is 'God is so good' (see page 17) translated into a few European languages:

- **French**: Mon Dieu est si bon (x 3), il est bon pour moi.
- **German**: Mein Gott ist so gut (x 3), er ist gut zu mir.
- **Spanish**: Dios es bueno (x 3), es bueno para mi.
- **Italian**: Dio è buono (x 3), è buono con me.

Prayers

Dearest Lord,
teach me to be generous;
teach me to serve you as you deserve;
to give and not to count the cost,
to fight and not to heed the wounds,
to toil and not to seek for rest,
to labour and not to ask for reward
save that of knowing I am doing your will.

ST IGNATIUS OF LOYOLA (SPAIN)

Hail Mary, full of grace, the Lord is with thee. Blessed are thou among women and blessed is the fruit of thy womb Jesus. Holy Mary, Mother of God, pray for us sinners now and at the hour of our death. Amen

HAIL MARY: A TRADITIONAL CATHOLIC PRAYER

Eternal God, the refuge and help of all your children,
we praise you for all you have given us,
for all you have done for us,
for all that you are to us.
In our weakness, you are strength,
in our darkness, you are light,
in our sorrow, you are comfort and peace.
We cannot number your blessings;
we cannot declare your love:
for all your blessings we bless you.
May we live as in your presence,
and love the things that you love,
and serve you in our daily lives;
through Jesus Christ our Lord.

ST BONIFACE, THE APOSTLE OF THE GERMANS

In Romania

A bird's-eye view of the church in Romania

Tradition claims that it was the apostle Andrew who first brought the gospel to Romania. The first Romanian Bible was produced in 1688.

Christmas night 1989 saw the downfall of Nicola Ceausescu, the former Communist President of Romania. Ceausescu's policy of encouraging his people to have big families led to a large number of unwanted children who, until recently, were being brought up in very crowded and under-resourced orphanages.

Most Romanian Christians are of the **Orthodox** tradition and, despite persecution and severe restrictions on church work during the communist years, today large numbers still attend church.

Orthodox churches don't traditionally have much seating; services are long but very colourful, and the worship space is full of special religious art called **icons**. These icons are pictures of Jesus and the stories from the Bible as well as the saints; they are an important aid to worship and prayer. There is a great sense of majesty and mystery in the symbols, pictures, colours, sounds and smells that are used in Orthodox services.

The Eastern and Oriental Orthodox churches form one of the three great Christian traditions, alongside Roman Catholics and Protestants. The emphasis on 'right worship' (which is the meaning of 'Orthodox') has roots that go back into the early centuries of the church. It is characteristic of the Orthodox to give priority to liturgy, and so they see mission as the invitation to all people to join with them in the unchanging worship of God, who is three-in-one.

Orthodox believers have had to survive many pressures down the years, including hostile political systems such as that of communist Russia. Today there are over 200 million believers from the Orthodox tradition, found mainly in 25 'family' groupings around the Middle East, Egypt, Ethiopia, across the CIS and in the former communist countries of Eastern Europe. Orthodox churches have also taken the lead in movements towards Christian unity, with the Greek and Indian Orthodox churches being among the founder members of the World Council of Churches.

The Orthodox cross is distinctive in that there is usually an additional cross-piece on the bottom half of the upright; this is where Jesus' feet would have been nailed. There is also an extra cross-piece at the top, where the title 'Jesus of Nazareth, King of the Jews' was written in three languages.

Questions and discussion starters

- Why do you think some Christians like to have special pictures, candlelight and the smell of incense to help them worship?
- What do you think about these features of a church service?
- How do you think the people of Romania managed to stay Christian when their communist government opposed all that they believed in?
- Find an icon of Jesus on the internet. What do you think about this special form of Christian art?
- Orthodox Christians will often make the sign of the cross over themselves when they are worshipping. Why do you think this sign is so important to Christians?
- Many Christians in the UK sent help to Romania when the communist era came to an end. Many churches and schools still send shoeboxes with basic provisions for poor children and families in Eastern Europe every Christmas time. Find out more about Christian partnership with this part of the world.
- Here is a useful link: www.smileinternational.org. If the children in Romania were to send you a shoebox as an expression of their love for you, what would you like them to put in it?

A simple song

Here is 'God is so good' (see page 17) translated into Romanian:

- Domnul este bun (x 3), este bun pentru noi.

Prayers

O Heavenly King, Comforter, Spirit of Truth;
Present in all places and filling all things;
Treasury of blessings and Giver of life;
Come and dwell in us and cleanse us from every impurity
and, of your goodness, save our souls.

AN ORTHODOX PRAYER

O Lord and Master of my life,
take from me the spirit of laziness, cowardice, greed and empty talk;
and give rather the spirit of love, humility and patience to your servant.
Grant, Lord, that I might see my own mistakes and not judge others,
for you are blessed for ever and ever. Amen

AN ORTHODOX PRAYER

In Israel/Palestine

A bird's-eye view of the church in the holy lands

The holy lands of Israel, Lebanon and Palestine are the birthplace of the Christian story. Many of the place names in these countries can still be recognised as the towns and cities where stories from the Bible took place—for example, Tyre and Sidon, Gaza and Nazareth, Jericho and, of course, Jerusalem.

The Jewish nation was dispersed across the world after the destruction of their capital city and their temple by the Romans, and the land became the home of many invaders alongside the local Palestinian people for centuries. Palestinian Christians claim that they can trace their roots right back to the time of Jesus.

Relationships between Muslims, Christians and Jews were usually good during this time. However, in the Middle Ages, the Crusades brought armies from Europe, intent on recapturing Jerusalem for the Christian Church. This resulted in much bloodshed and sowed deep mistrust and hatred between the three 'Faiths of the Book'.

After World War II, the State of Israel was re-established in the region (in 1948), but land had to be taken from the local Palestinian people, who were mainly Muslim but included Christian groups too. This has caused fear and civil unrest. At the time of writing, a security wall exists to separate the faith communities and reconciliation and peace seem a long way off.

The Gaza Strip is the most populated piece of land on earth. After the United Nations Partition Plan, thousands of Palestinians, expelled from villages along the coastal plains, sought refuge in Gaza. The world Palestinian population is almost 8 million. Two-thirds of these people are refugees in other countries. 92 per cent of the land that became Israel was originally Palestine. Many Palestinians live in refugee camps, which, after 40 years, have become permanent 'homes'.

Many Christians from around the world still like to make pilgrimages to the holy lands, to walk in the footsteps of Jesus. However, security issues in recent years have made this more difficult. Many local Christians are moving out of the region, if they can afford it, hoping to make new lives for themselves in the West.

Nevertheless, Christians still make up about 30 per cent of the population of the Lebanon. The largest Christian group here is the Maronites, whose Christian tradition goes back to the fifth century after Christ. Jesus visited Lebanon and healed a woman's daughter (Matthew 15:21–28). He called her a woman of great faith.

Elijah hid in Lebanon when he was on the run from King Ahab, and he too helped a woman there and healed her son (1 Kings 17).

The Arabic word for forgiveness and reconciliation is 'musalaha'. An interfaith group using that name regularly brings together young people from all three faith traditions of the region, to help them begin to understand each other and work together.

Embrace the Middle East is a Christian charity working among disadvantaged people in this region and can provide further useful background: visit www.embraceme.org.

Michael Morpurgo's book *The Kites are Flying!* (Walker, 2009) is a moving story that explores the fears and hopes of this region.

Questions and discussion starters

- What other faith groups meet in the community near your school?
- What do you know about them?
- What things do you think they all might have in common?
- I wonder what Jesus would say today about the current situation in the land of his birth.
- Why do you think it is so hard for some people of different faiths to get on with each other?
- The Christians who are still in the holy lands often feel forgotten by the rest of the Christian world. How might Western Christians do more to help them?
- Reconciliation between people who mistrust or even hate each other isn't easy. What are your top tips for getting on with people who are very different from yourself?
- Print off a map of the holy lands and see how many names of Bible places you can spot. Can you find out which Bible stories happened there?
- Jerusalem is a sacred city for Jews, Muslims and Christians. Do you think it is ever possible to share something that is so special?

A simple song

Here is the song 'Hallelu, hallelu' (*Junior Praise* 67) in Arabic (shown with English lettering). 'Hallelujah' is Hebrew for 'Praise God'.

This song is often sung with actions, one half singing the hallelujahs and the other the words in bold below, standing whenever it is their turn to sing.

Hallelu, Hallelu, Hallelu, Hallelujah
Shokran lelrub. *(Thanks to the Lord)*
Hallelu, Hallelu, Hallelu, Hallelujah
Shokran lelrub.
Shokran lelrub, *Hallelujah [x 3]*
Shokran lelrub.

You could also use the following words:

- Hamdan lelrub (Praise to the Lord)
- Magdan lelrub (Glory to the Lord)
- Haigi tani elrub (The Lord is coming soon)

Prayers

On the eve of Christmas, hatred will vanish;
On the eve of Christmas, the earth will flourish;
On the eve of Christmas, war will be gone;
On the eve of Christmas, love will be born.
When we offer a glass of water to a thirsty person, it is Christmas;
When we clothe a naked person with a gown of love, it is Christmas;
When we wipe the tears from weeping eyes, it is Christmas;
When we line a hopeless heart with love, it is Christmas.

ARABIC SONG (TRANSLATED)

Lord, after all the talking, questioning and agonising over your land, grant that some compassionate breakthrough may occur. Amen

PRAYER FROM THE MIDDLE EAST

Strengthen those, O Lord, who thirst for mercy and justice but have been deprived of the right to live in dignity. For such are those you have loved, reminding us that they are our neighbours. Free them from oppression; restore to them the right to life and to independence in their own land, just as other nations enjoy this right. Amen

PRAYER FROM JERUSALEM

In Southern Sudan

A bird's-eye view of the church in the Sudan

Life in Sudan revolves around the great River Nile, which divides the country north to south. It was along the course of this river that the news of Jesus first travelled to Sudan. Later, it was also the route taken by the Arabs who brought Islam to northern Sudan in particular. However, some Sudanese claim that their links to the story of the Bible go back much further, believing that the Queen of Sheba, who visited King Solomon, came from their country (2 Chronicles 9:1–12).

The majority of people in this region are Arabic and Muslim, but in the south there is a large Christian population among the African tribes. In July 2010, South Sudan became an independent country, but it is one of the poorest in the world.

The first Anglican mission was opened in 1899 at Omdurman.

Civil war between the north and south lasted for most of the second half of the last century, and many southern Sudanese were forced to escape as refugees to other countries. There are still groups in exile in parts of Africa, the Middle East and also in the UK.

The war brought displacement and loss of life, causing untold damage to the traditional culture of the people. School and family life was disrupted and crops and cattle destroyed. Despite the war and the suffering, the Christian church in the south has grown. There are new songs of worship and a great desire to teach and share the Christian faith. Their ebony crosses, decorated with spent cartridge cases from the fighting, are symbolic of the triumph of their Christian faith in the face of suffering. (For more details about this cross, see *A-cross the World*, Barnabas, 2004.)

In South Sudan and in refugee camps elsewhere, mission agencies are helping to train new leaders for this growing church.

Questions and discussion starters

- Many Sudanese churches were destroyed in the civil war, but do you think there might be advantages to meeting out of doors—under the shade of a tree, for example?
- Many Sudanese Christians were forced to run away from their homes. If you had to leave your home in a hurry, what few belongings would you want to keep with you?
- What could others do to help you?
- What would you most miss about home?
- The Christians in South Sudan created a special cross from what they had to hand. What special symbol would you make, to help you hold on to hope when the future looked bleak?
- The story of Jesus is clearly not important to Christians just in the good times of life. What do you think it is about this faith that keeps people believing even when everything has gone wrong? (Maybe you can invite a Christian into your school and ask him or her about this.)
- Do you know of any refugee groups who live in your community?
- Soon after his birth, Jesus himself became a refugee with his family in Egypt (Matthew 2:13–15). How might this be a helpful story for Christians from Sudan?
- Do you think that when we have to go through hard times, it is possible that we learn more about ourselves, others and God than if everything always went smoothly?

A simple song

Here is the song 'God is so good' (see page 17) in the Dinka language, which is one of many spoken in Sudan.

Ngun a lo'but (x 3),
lepeng nyanyar nan.

Prayers

We ask you, God of all peoples,
'Who has created us?'
Isn't it you who created us, God of all peoples?
Listen to the prayers rising from our bones in the wilderness.
Watch over us, our Creator,
And we beg you to liberate us.
Hear the prayer of our souls in the wilderness.
God of all people, we yearn for peace in our land,
That we may pray to you in freedom:
This is the prayer we make:
Hear our prayers as we cry out to you,
Hear the wailing of our souls in the wilderness.
Watch over us, our Creator.

A DINKA POEM

Come, everyone, and beg God to give life to humankind,
Come, everyone, and receive life from God.
Rain mixed with sunbeams will give us life.

A DINKA PRAYER

Our Father, it is your universe,
It is your will; let us be at peace.
Let the souls of your people be cool.
You are our Father; remove all evil from our path.

A NUER PRAYER

There is material for a lesson and collective worship linked to Archbishop Janani Luwum on the Barnabas in Schools website:

www.barnabasinschools.org.uk/janani-lawum-from-uganda-17-february/

Further information about the churches in this part of east Africa can be found at www.cms-uk.org.

In Uganda

A bird's-eye view of the church in Uganda

Uganda is bordered by Sudan, Kenya, Tanzania, Rwanda and the Democratic Republic of the Congo.

The largest area of fresh water in Africa, Lake Victoria, lies in the south-east of Uganda.

Uganda's capital is Kampala. On Namirembe Hill (the name means 'the place of peace') is the city's cathedral along with Mengo Mission Hospital.

In 1962, Uganda became a state in her own right within the Commonwealth after some 70 years of British rule. The Anglican Church of Uganda is over 130 years old.

Ugandan Christians have known suffering and persecution. In 1884, the missionary Bishop James Hannington was killed along with his African porters. Some years later, young converts faced death by being burned alive and are remembered today as the first African **martyrs**. In 1977, Archbishop Janani Luwum was murdered because he spoke out bravely against the injustice of the government of his day.

Mission agencies still partner the Anglican Church of Uganda, supporting its involvement in theological training, education, medical work and community development. There are also many fast-growing African independent churches.

The north-east of Uganda is known as the Karamoja. This is largely desert, inhabited by a nomadic people with their cattle. In recent years this region has been badly affected by fighting that has been particularly brutal and cruel, sadly often involving the recruitment of child soldiers.

Almost every Ugandan family has been affected in some way by the AIDS pandemic, which the Ugandan people call 'slim'. There are many children who have been orphaned, and many are looked after by grandparents or even in child-headed households.

The church in Uganda experienced a period of particular renewal and growth in the 1930s. The theme song of this revival was 'Tukutendereza' (we praise you).

Although much of the worship in the mainstream churches was, for a long time, greatly influenced by its Anglican roots, nowadays local instruments and exuberance in worship are being incorporated.

Questions and discussion starters

- What musical instruments are used in the churches you know about?
- Do you think that some types of music are better suited to the worship of God than others?
- What do you think about using dance or clapping in worship? Read what King David did when he got excited about God (2 Samuel 6:12–19).
- The church in Uganda is still young within the global history of Christianity. What insights do you think it might have to share with older parts of the Christian family?
- Some of the Christians in northern parts of Uganda have faced much suffering but are still prepared to forgive their enemies. Do you think some things are unforgivable? How is it that some Christians have found the strength to forgive?
- How far would you be prepared to go when standing up for what was fair in the face of threats and even a danger to your life?

A simple song

Here is the song 'God is so good' (see page 17) in some of the languages of this region of Africa.

- **Rukiga (South-west Uganda)**: Ruhanga ni murungi (x 3), ni murungi wangye.
- **Swahili**: Mungu ni mwema (x 3), ni mwema wangu.
- **Kirundi (Burundi)**: Yemw' l-mana (x 3), yacu ni nzi-za.

Prayers

Keep us, God, from panic, when crises and panics arise.
Help us to know that though you do not always remove troubles from us,
you always accompany us through them. Amen

A PRAYER FROM UGANDA

May God clean my heart, as I clean my town.

A PRAYER FROM UGANDA

Have mercy on us, Lord,
and on AIDS sufferers throughout the world.
Love and compassion to all who seek
to assist them,
Through Jesus Christ our Lord. Amen

FROM A PRAYER WRITTEN BY BISHOP MISAERI KAUMA OF UGANDA

In South Africa

A bird's-eye view of the church in South Africa

After the first Dutch settlers arrived in South Africa in 1652, Protestant Christianity, through the Dutch Reformed Church, held total monopoly until the 19th century.

Today, some three-quarters of the black population are members of 'protestant' churches. This figure includes a majority of African-initiated/independent churches and Pentecostals. In 1908, South Africa was one of the first countries on the continent to embrace Pentecostalism.

South Africa lies on the important trade route between the Atlantic and Indian Oceans, which has meant that many empires have laid claim to this land over the centuries, most recently the Dutch and the British. These groups sought in different ways to subdue the indigenous black peoples of the land and this developed into a political policy of **apartheid**, which, sadly, was justified by some Christians using verses from the Bible. It led to much unrest, injustice and bloodshed, particularly in the second half of the last century.

Increasingly the apartheid system was challenged both from within and through international boycotts. Leading Christian missionary priests like Trevor Huddleston, who worked in South Africa before returning to the UK, campaigned for change, while local Christian leaders such as Archbishop Desmond Tutu worked tirelessly for a new South Africa where everyone was treated equally, inspired by the truths of the Christian gospel (see Galatians 3:28–29).

The release of the imprisoned leader Nelson Mandela in 1990 heralded a new beginning for South Africa as a new 'rainbow nation'. People worked hard to heal the divisions of the apartheid years and Archbishop Tutu chaired the famous Truth and Justice Commission, where victims and persecutors came face to face in a process of reconciliation.

South Africa still faces many problems, including great inequality of wealth and much violence. However, the Christian churches are trying to demonstrate the unity and integration of the races that can be possible.

For further information about the Anglican Church in South Africa, go to www.uspg.org.uk. For information on all the churches, visit www.oikoumene.org/en/member-churches/regions/africa/south-africa.html.

Questions and discussion starters

- To what degree is your school and community a 'rainbow nation' of different ethnic groups?
- If there are not many different ethnic groups, what do you think you might be missing?
- What are the advantages and challenges of bringing different ethnic groups together?
- Why do you think people develop prejudices against those who are different from themselves?
- What is your solution for tackling prejudice?
- What can churches do, in your opinion, to bring people together?
- Find out more about Nelson Mandela and his contribution to making the new South Africa. What prejudices did he have to overcome?
- When Jesus lived in Judea, he challenged prejudice and the 'apartheid' of his day. Read about how he dealt with outsiders such as Samaritans, lepers and a Roman officer (see Luke 5:12–16; 7:1–10 and 9:51–56).
- How would you go about bringing together two people who were enemies, with the aim of mending the rifts between them?
- Desmond Tutu said, 'Do your little bit of good where you are; it's those little bits of good put together that overwhelm the world.' How can this be applied to a classroom, a school, a community or a church?
- What teaches you more: encountering things that are the same or things that are different? Can this apply to people too?

A simple song

Here is the song 'God is so good' (see page 17) in one of the languages of South Africa.

- **Afrikaans**: God is so goed (x 3), Hy is goed vir my.

Another South African language is Xhosa. The song 'We are marching in the light of God' in this language goes:

Siyahamb' ekukhanyen Kew-nkhos

The words to this song can be found on the website www.barnabasinschools.org.uk/whereintheworld/, along with an mp3 file.

Prayers

O God, we are in great darkness.
When we heard of Jesus
we saw a light afar off.
Do not let anything put out that light
but lead us nearer to it. Amen

AN AFRICAN PRAYER

You asked for my hands
that you might use them for your purpose.
I gave them for a moment,
but then withdrew them, for the work was hard.

You asked for my mouth
to speak out against injustice.
I gave you a whisper, that I might not be accused.

You asked for eyes to see the pain of poverty.
I closed them, for I did not want to see.

You asked for my life,
that you might work through me.
I gave you a small part,
that I might not get too involved.

Lord, forgive me for my calculated efforts
to serve you
Only when it is convenient for me to do so,
Only in those places where it is safe to do so
And only with those who make it easy to do so.

Father, forgive me,
renew me,
and send me out
as a usable instrument,
that I might take seriously
the meaning of your cross.

JOE SEREMANE, SOUTH AFRICA

Chapter 3

From somewhere to everywhere

Overview of content

What follows is a brief account of how the church grew so large, ending with a focus on the story of Pentecost that includes age-specific presentation suggestions for the classroom or collective worship.

How the Christian Church began and grew

The first followers of Jesus were convinced that Jesus had come back to life after his death on a cross on the first Good Friday. It was impossible for them to keep silent about this, as, for them, it was proof positive that Jesus was the way to God and that death was not the end.

On the day that Jesus left them to go back to heaven, he gave them instructions about what to do. Christians call that day Ascension Day. Jesus said, 'The Holy Spirit will come upon you and give you power. Then you will tell everyone about me in Jerusalem, in all Judea, in Samaria, and everywhere in the world' (Acts 1:8).

The first travellers with this story were the disciples chosen by Jesus. They began where they lived and then took the message out into the world in ever-widening circles. During the following centuries, the Christian faith was passed on from person to person and country to country, like a baton in a global relay race. The story of Jesus spread rapidly and, very soon, churches were established across the Middle East, in Europe, north Africa, India and even further east. All this was happening before the message of Christianity ever first properly reached the shores of Britain.

Here is a snapshot of how the church grew in those early centuries:

From Jerusalem to Rome

In his book the Acts of the Apostles, in the New Testament, Luke records the story of how the Christian faith spread around the eastern and central Mediterranean.

Peter, one of Jesus' closest friends, became a leader of the church and had many missionary adventures, including escapes from prison and encounters with non-Jews who increasingly began to accept the Christian faith.

Alongside this story, Luke introduces us to Saul from modern-day Turkey, who had an amazing encounter with Jesus in a vision on his way to Damascus. He had been an orthodox Jew, opposed to Christianity, but experienced a complete change of heart. Using his Roman name, *Paul*, he became the leading missionary evangelist, establishing churches throughout modern Turkey and Greece. Acts 21 records the exciting story of his final journey by ship to Rome as a prisoner. Accused of sedition by his enemies back in Judea, he had appealed to be tried before Caesar. He ended up under house arrest in the capital of the greatest empire of the time. His many letters, also in the New Testament, became widely read and helped Christians understand more about who Jesus was and how they should live their lives, filled with God's Holy Spirit.

Tradition has it that Paul and Peter met in Rome, where they were both eventually executed. At this stage, Christianity was seen as a strange and dangerous sect that needed to be suppressed. The Christians had to be very secretive about their faith, but this didn't stop the story of Jesus from spreading.

- You can read about Peter's experience of God on the day of Pentecost in Acts 2:1–4 and 22–36, and his miraculous prison escape in Acts 12:6–17.
- You can read about Paul's amazing conversion in Acts 9:1–25, and his dramatic shipwreck in Acts 27:13–44.

From Jerusalem to Ethiopia

Luke also records in Acts the intriguing story of the royal treasurer from Ethiopia, who had come to Jerusalem to worship God. He was returning in his chariot when he met *Philip*, one of the first deacons appointed by the Christian Church. He was reading some words by the prophet Isaiah, which he couldn't understand. Philip explained that the passage referred to Jesus, and this gave him the opportunity to tell him the whole story of Jesus' life, death and resurrection. There and then, the Ethopian official was **baptised** and took the story and his new faith back to his own country. Ethiopians today trace their country's Christian roots back to this one man.

- You can read about this story in Acts 8:26–40.
- You can see what the treasurer was reading in Isaiah 53.

From Jerusalem to the Ukraine (and Scotland)

Another of the disciples was *Andrew*, Peter's brother. He is also said to have travelled far with the story of Jesus—in fact, to the far north of the known world at that time. Tradition claims that Andrew went through modern-day Turkey, along the Black Sea and then north to the River Volga and what is now Ukraine. Several countries in Eastern Europe today lay claim to his missionary activities and even Russia has adopted him as a patron saint. He is said to have died in Greece, crucified like Jesus but on a distinctive X-shaped cross.

Andrew's link to Scotland arises because his **relics** were taken there in the sixth century by monks on a mission to share the good news about Jesus. The place where he was reburied is the site of the present-day city of St Andrews. Andrew seems to have been a great traveller and, ever since the middle of the 19th century, St Andrew's day (30 November) has been used as a special time of prayer for world mission.

- You can read how enthusiastic Andrew was to tell his brother about Jesus in John 1:40–42.

From Jerusalem to India

Another of Jesus' disciples was *Thomas*, who is said to have travelled to India to share the Christian story, as early as the middle of the first century AD. Crossing the Red Sea and then the Persian Gulf, tradition claims that he landed in a place called Kerala on the Malabar coast. Even today, many Christians in that region belong to the Mar Thoma Church, which is named after him. A distinctive St Thomas' cross is commonly seen in India, often worn on a long pendant around the neck.

- You can read how Thomas was the first disciple truly to recognise that Jesus was God on earth, in John 20:24–29.

From everywhere to everywhere

In this way the Christian story has continued to be passed on from country to country over the 2000 years since the events surrounding the life and death of Jesus Christ. Some of the stories of individuals involved in this worldwide movement are recorded in Chapter 8.

In the 21st century, the story of the Christian faith continues to be an 'everywhere to everywhere' sharing. The last century in particular saw a dramatic shift in the centre of gravity of the Christian world. The church in 'the south'—Latin America, Africa and parts of Asia—is now growing rapidly, in contrast to the 'old church' of Europe and North America. Most modern missionaries are coming from places like Nigeria, India and South Korea. At the same time, the old world of the north and west is where power and wealth mainly lie. The average world Christian in its present-day two-billion-strong family of faith is black, poor, male and most likely out of work.

A big challenge

All this is a big challenge for Christians in the 21st century. What can the churches of Europe and America learn from the new vibrant churches of the south that will help reignite Christian discipleship in its largely secular societies? What lessons have the churches of the north learned over their 2000 years of history that they could share with their youthful and passionate brothers and sisters in the south? How might they use their wealth and influence to challenge and change the terrible imbalance in the world's resources? The World Council of Churches and other similar international Christian organisations and conferences try to address just these issues.

The growing churches in the poorer parts of the world are often leading the way in waking up Christians to many pressing global concerns about justice, the environment and unfair trade. At the same time, they are challenging the traditional church to find new ways to share the story of Jesus in this generation.

Working together

In the New Testament, Paul uses the picture of a human body to remind Christians that the Church is bigger than they realise and is made up of many parts (1 Corinthians 12:12–27). This passage is usually applied only to single congregations whose members each have their own unique and vital gifts; however, it applies equally well to the worldwide Christian family.

If Paul had been writing his letter today, he might have written the following version:

For just as the body is one and has many members, so all the members of the Church, though many, are one Church. So it is with Christ. For by one Spirit we were all baptised into one Church: Europeans, Africans, Asians—all were made to drink of one Spirit.

The church in Uganda cannot say, 'Because I am not English, I do not belong to the world Church.' If the whole Church were European, where would be the enthusiasm?

There are many parts, yet one Church. The church in Latin America cannot say to the church in Mozambique, 'I have no need of you.' Nor can the church in China say to the church in Nepal, 'I have no need of you.'

God has so blessed the Church that the members may have the same care for one another. If one part of the world Church suffers, all suffer. If one part of the world Church is honoured, all rejoice together.

You are a world Church, the body of Christ, and each one of you is a part of it.

Focusing on Pentecost

Here are two ideas for exploring the festival of Pentecost with your class or as a special presentation for an assembly.

Activity: Re-enacting the story (7-11 years)

Pentecost celebrates the birthday of the Church. It was the day when Jesus fulfilled his promise of sending his followers the Spirit of God to be with them and in them. It happened 50 days after the events of Easter and coincided with the Jewish harvest festival of Shevuot.

This coming of God as the Holy Spirit was marked by the sounds and signs of God's power, which enabled them to carry out the task of taking the good news to the ends of the earth. Christians believe that God's Spirit still empowers Christians today to share and show the love of God. The promise was for young and old, men and women and children. The story is found in Acts 2.

The following outline is a way of presenting the story, in which the whole class can take part.

Preparation

You will need various sizes of thick stiff card; orange, red and yellow ribbons; large placards with various words of praise (see below); words on cards and on overheads for individual readers and the class (see below); small flame shapes, pencils/crayons; a large Pentecost flame for prayers.

Presentation

Introduce the theme by showing a birthday cake with a small number of candles. Make links to any birthdays in the class around this time. Pentecost is a birthday, and there ought to be about 2000 candles. Pentecost is the birthday of the Christian Church.

Begin the presentation with a time of quiet and then introduce some reflective music in the background as you listen to the following promises of Jesus about the gift of the Spirit.

'If you love me, you will do as I command. Then I will ask the Father to send you the Holy Spirit who will help you and always be with you.' (John 14:15–16)

'The Spirit shows what is true and will come and guide you into the full truth.' (John 16:13)

'Have faith in me, and you will have life-giving water flowing from deep inside you, just as the Scriptures say.' Jesus was talking about the Holy Spirit, who would be given to everyone that had faith in him. The Spirit had not yet been given to anyone, since Jesus had not yet been given his full glory. (John 7:38–39)

Jesus breathed on them and said, 'Receive the Holy Spirit.' (John 20:22)

'I will send you the one my Father has promised, but you must stay in the city until you are given power from heaven.' (Luke 24:49)

The outward signs of the Spirit's coming were the sound of a strong wind, the appearance of flames, and the ability to speak God's praise in new languages. Read Acts 2:1–4, dramatising it with the following effects.

- Arrange one group of children to be ready with pieces of stiff card of varying sizes, with which they can create a breeze (or a stronger wind) as they wave them towards the rest of the class or audience.
- Arrange a second group of children to be ready with yellow, red and orange ribbons, with which they can create flame effects as they wave them over the rest of the class or audience.
- Arrange a third group of children to be ready with words of praise on placards in four languages, with which they can lead the rest of the class in a repeated and ever louder chorus of international praise. Suggested phrases might be:

  * Demos gloria al senor (Spanish)
  * Isus e minunat (Romanian)

* Bwana Asifiwe (Swahili)
* Stuti Hoos Prabhu (Hindi)

After you have read the passage with the sound effects, allow a pause for silence and then play some thoughtful music while the class share in the crowd's response of 'What does this mean?' In Acts, it was Peter who helped explain to them what they were witnessing. Unpack the meaning in a similar way, using a group of children (reading in chorus) to make Peter's first key points (Acts 2:14–21):

- This is what God promised would happen.
- It was all predicted long ago in the scriptures.
- God wants to live inside his people by his Spirit.
- The Holy Spirit is a gift for all—young and old, rich and poor, women and men.
- Whoever calls on God can experience all this because of what Jesus did.

Peter went on to focus on Jesus—the story of his life, death and resurrection (vv. 22–36). This could be explored by asking the class or audience, in groups, to come up with anything they remember about the life of Jesus.

The reaction of the people in Acts was to ask, 'What shall we do?' Ask the class or audience to turn to those sitting near them, in groups of three and four, and to put themselves into the shoes of the crowd at the first Pentecost. Display the following questions for them to talk over in their groups.

- I wonder what the crowds really thought was happening that morning.
- I wonder what most impressed the crowds.
- I wonder what the crowds thought of Peter and his words.
- I wonder what they thought Peter would say next.

Listen to some of the responses from the groups, then read together what Peter said next, from Acts 2:38–39.

Christians believe that the same gift of the Holy Spirit is also for believers today, if they do what Peter says, both receiving God's forgiveness through Jesus and opening their lives to the work of the Holy Spirit.

Follow the presentation with some international Christian singing, such as the simple song suggested in Chapter 2 ('God is so good' in different languages) or one of the songs linked to this book on the website, www.barnabasinschools.org.uk/whereintheworld/

Ask the whole class to write a word or draw a picture on small flame shapes to express what they feel about Pentecost. They can then bring the flame shapes up to the front and stick them on to a large Holy Spirit flame, while some appropriate music is playing.

Questions for discussion and response

- What difference did the Holy Spirit make at Pentecost? Read what happened in Acts 2:41–47.
- What difference does the Holy Spirit make for Christians today? Use some of the stories from this chapter about how the church grew.

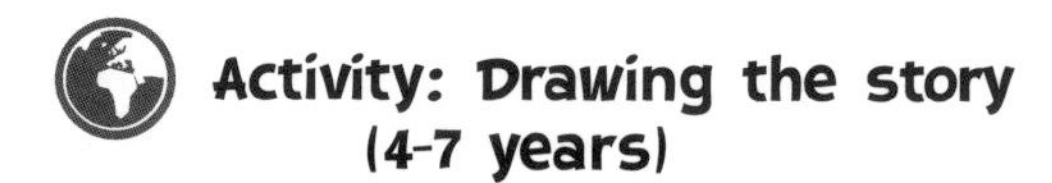

Activity: Drawing the story (4–7 years)

The idea of this outline is to connect the Pentecost story to other Bible stories to show how Christians believe that God's plan for a worldwide Church stretches back across the centuries.

NB: If you are using this outline as a talk in an assembly, you will do all the drawing yourself. With a class group, the children could do the drawing themselves as you talk together. They will also make their own links to other stories.

Preparation

You will need a large sheet of paper and coloured pens. Draw a wide border around the edge of the paper and draw five circles on the paper.

Development

Tell the story of Pentecost as follows.

It was the Festival of Shavuot or Pentecost, when Jews would come from all over the world to Jerusalem to celebrate together.

Inside the border of the whole sheet of paper, draw adults and children of all races and colours, smiling and running in towards the centre.

What were they celebrating? It was the harvest festival—the time when they would bring offerings of the first of the crops to God and decorate the houses with flowers, as we do in church in the autumn.

In one circle, draw as many sorts of fruit and vegetable and grain as you can think of.

Shavuot was also the festival to celebrate the time when God gave Moses the Law—the Ten Commandments. Can you remember them?

In another circle, draw the stone tablets and talk about what the Commandments are.

On this particular Shavuot or Pentecost festival, the one after Jesus had died and come back to life and gone to be with God, his disciples were together in Jerusalem. Suddenly there was a noise like a strong wind from heaven and it filled the whole house where they were.

Fill a circle with swirls of colour for the wind.

As well as the wind, something like flames of fire separated and came to rest on each person there.

Fill a circle with flames.

They were filled with the Holy Spirit and began to speak in different languages. The people who heard them, who came from many different countries, were amazed to hear them speaking every one of their own languages.

Fill a circle with as many words or random letters as the group knows.

Peter, filled with the Holy Spirit, told the crowds who Jesus was, and about 3000 people started to believe in Jesus that very day.

Now think about these circles. How can we move in and out of them? Look at the harvest circle. Why do you think God chose a harvest festival to give out his Spirit?

Paul wrote, 'God's Spirit makes us loving, happy, peaceful, patient, kind, good, faithful, gentle and self-controlled' (Galatians 5:22–23). Christians call these the 'fruit of the Spirit'—they're good things that grow in us when we love God.

Write the words in a bigger circle around the harvest circle.

Look at the law circle. Why do you think God chose the time when the people remembered God's law to give them his Holy Spirit?

Christians believe that God can now put his law into people's hearts (Jeremiah 31:33). This makes them want to keep it as the Holy Spirit changes them to make them more like Jesus.

Draw hearts around the law circle.

Look at the wind circle. Where else do we hear about wind in the Bible? The first book of the Bible, Genesis, talks about the breath of God, or God's Spirit, moving over the waters of creation. At Pentecost, God is making a new creation.

Draw the world and other symbols of creation around the wind circle.

Look at the fire circle. Where else do we read of fire in the Bible? When the Israelites escaped from Egypt across the desert, God guided them at night with a pillar of fire (Exodus 13:21). Christians believe that a guiding light can be put into people's hearts so they can know which way God wants them to go.

Draw signposts round the fiery circle.

Look at the language circle. When in the Bible did languages tear people apart? In the book of Genesis, we can read how people tried to build a tower reaching as high as heaven, called the Tower of Babel. At that time, God stopped the people from building any higher by mixing up their languages (Genesis 11:7), but now the Holy Spirit can bring different people and races together again.

Draw lines from each of the border characters, leading to the language circle.

I wonder what you like best about the Holy Spirit in this picture of Pentecost.

Chapter 4

Everywhere a celebration

Overview of content

This chapter and the three chapters that follow give insights into how Christians worship in church and celebrate key festivals, with practical resources for the classroom and collective worship.

Worship around the world

The Christian faith is the most widely spread of the world's great faiths and it has proved to be remarkably adaptable. Wherever it has taken root and grown, local Christians have always gathered regularly to worship God using their own languages and elements from their indigenous cultures.

Of course, there have been times when the Christian story wasn't allowed to be inculturated properly like this. There are many uncomfortable examples, even today, of places where the story of Jesus has been received but wrapped up in particular cultural clothing, which does not fit new believers who are living with very different circumstances and cultural norms. Cumbersome Anglican robes for priests, for example, don't make a lot of sense in equatorial regions, and the notion that an organ is the best instrument for divine worship is hard to sustain in a climate where its mechanics will soon fail and there is no one to repair it.

Bible translators wrestle with similar challenges, as words that make sense in one context do not convey the same meaning in another language. A word like 'carry' may seem simple enough in English, but, in the language of a tribal culture that has many different words for 'carry', depending on the context and the style of carrying, it is really important to translate a verse correctly if the true meaning is to be conveyed.

The following chapters gather together some examples of how contemporary Christians in other countries approach their regular worship and their special festival celebrations. There are many ideas that can be drawn on to bring a global dimension into an assembly or church service or as examples for discussion within a lesson on how Christians worship God.

The apostle to the Alaskans
During the 19th century, St Innocent worked for 45 years as a missionary in Siberia and Alaska, which was then part of greater Russia. He had to think very carefully when trying to translate the Bible in a way that would make sense to the Inuit people of the Arctic. They knew nothing of grazing animals, so descriptions of Jesus as the 'lamb of God' would be meaningless. In their Bible, Jesus becomes 'the baby seal of God', for the seal is an animal they know and understand. In fact, they depend on it for food, clothing and fuel: it is their life.

The following areas are covered:

- The welcome
- The call to worship
- Passing the Peace
- Saying prayers
- Baptism
- Communion
- Celebrating harvest
- Celebrating Christmas
- Celebrating Easter

Examples of seven songs from around the world can be found at the website www.barnabasinschools.org.uk/whereintheworld/. The website also gives a link to a further collection of world songs.

*****

One of the most effective ways to help children and adults to step into Christian worship from around the world is by using religious artwork from different cultures. There is a huge amount available now on the internet. There are also specific packs of artwork for schools. Here is a list of online and published material that you may find helpful:

- *The Image of Christ*, Gabriele Finaldi (National Gallery, 2011), available from www.nationalgallery.co.uk
- *Christ for All People: Celebrating a world of Christian art*, Ron O'Grady (Orbis Books, 2001)
- *Picturing Jesus: Worldwide contemporary artists* (Pack B), Latimer Blaylock (CEP, 2004)
- *Picturing Easter: Classroom explanation of the biblical story using art from Christian communities all across the globe*, Lat Blaylock and Victoria Ikwuemesi (CEP, 2008)
- *Picturing Jesus: Fresh ideas*, Lat Blaylock (CEP, 2009)
- *The Bible through Art,* Margaret Cooling (RMEP, 2000)
- *Jesus through Art,* Margaret Cooling (RMEP, 2000)
- *Christian Art,* Winitha Fernando (Fernando Publishers, 2008)
- *The Christian Story: Five Asian artists today,* Patricia C. Ponagracz et al. (Giles, 2007)
- *The Passion in Art,* Richard Harries (Ashgate, 2004)
- *Windows into Heaven: Icons and spirituality of Russia*, Simon Jenkins (Lion Hudson, 1998)
- *Black Angels: Art and spirituality of Ethiopia*, Richard Marsh (Lion Hudson, 1998)

- *Jesus Mafa* (images from West Africa): search at www.jesusmafa.com
- *Born Among Us* (study pack), available at www.uspg.org.uk
- *The Christ We Share: A world church resource for local mission*, available at www.cms-shop.org.uk

Chapter 5

Everywhere a service of worship

Overview of content

Today there is increasing variety in styles of Christian worship across the world. Among churches in countries that were founded by missionaries from the West, there are still many recognisable elements that are common to worship in local churches in the UK. However, as these churches have become independent, with indigenous leadership, local musical instruments and symbols, national characteristics and cultural preferences have become part of the mix. This chapter explores what this means as far as the welcome, the call to worship, the Peace and saying prayers are concerned. Each section includes activity suggestions that may be used in the classroom and/or collective worship.

World worship: the welcome

One of the most important aspects of any Christian church, wherever it is in the world, is the welcome that people give to each other and especially to outsiders.

Activity: Global 'hello'

Play this simple game using a selection of 24 words for 'hello' or 'welcome' from a variety of countries worldwide. The leader should spend some time becoming familiar with the list of greetings before introducing them to the children.

Write each greeting on two separate cards. Jumble up the cards and let the children select a card each. The children now have to find their 'partner' with the same greeting by going up to the others and using their greeting.

A follow-up activity with this material would be to create a class welcome poster using the various world greetings.

- From Sri Lanka: In Sinhalese, people greet each other with hands together as in prayer and a slight bow of the upper body. They say a word that sounds like '**Are-you-bow-an**'.

- From Japan: In Japanese, the greeting sounds like '**Kon-eechi-wa**'. Ohayo gozai-mass (or just 'Ohayo') means 'good morning'. Kom-ban wa means 'good evening'.

- From Eritrea: To greet someone, hold each other by the right hand and gently pull together, touching shoulders three times. The word to use would be the Arabic word for peace, pronounced '**Salaam**'.

- From Nigeria: There are a variety of different tribal greetings. Such greetings are usually accompanied by 'hand and thumb' shakes, with the other hand on the heart to emphasize sincerity or under the elbow of the person being greeted. These three all mean 'hello':
  - **Kedu**
  - **No** (short 'o')
  - **Kubay-obway**

- From Uganda: Again there are a variety of tribal greetings:
  - **Agandi** means 'hello'.
  - **Ku-tu-midde nyo** means 'greetings, how are you?'
  - **Kuthie** means 'hello'.

- From South Africa
  - **Sabona** is a Zulu 'hello', usually accompanied by an ordinary handshake, then a thumb- and hand-shake, then the ends of the fingers interlocked, the thumbs rubbing each other.
  - **Goeiemore**, pronounced 'Hoi-amora', means 'hello' in Afrikaans.
  - **Dumela** means 'hello' in Sotho

- From New Zealand: '**Tehi Mauria**' means 'I greet you'—literally, 'I salute the breath of life in you.' It is traditionally accompanied by rubbing noses.

- From Venezuela: '**Bendicion**', pronounced Ben-dís-ee-on, means 'a blessing please'. The customary reply is 'Dios te bendiga', pronounced Di-os tay ben-dee-ga, which means 'God bless you'.

- From Albania: '**Mira dita**' means 'good morning/ day'.
- From Lebanon: '**Ahlan, ahlan**', usually said with one hand on your heart, means 'Greetings, peace to you.'
- From Egypt: '**Zal-ak**', pronounced Zeye-ak, means 'welcome/hello'.
- From Nepal: '**Namaste**' is used in Nepal and in various forms throughout the Indian subcontinent. It means literally, 'I honour/respect you.'
- From East Africa: '**Jambo**', a common Swahili greeting, means 'hello'.
- From China: '**Ni hao ma**', a Chinese greeting whose roots lie in a phrase meaning 'Have you eaten yet?'
- From Romania: '**Domnul ajouta**', a Romanian greeting meaning literally 'The Lord be your helper'. Romanians also use 'Buna', which is a common everyday word for 'hello'.
- From the Arabic-speaking world: '**Sab(ah) achir**', an Arabic greeting meaning 'peace be with you'. The Arabic for 'welcome to you' is pronounced 'Marhaban bik', with a breathed 'h', such as when you breathe on to a mirror to polish it.
- From Pakistan: '**Salaam ji**', a greeting heard particularly among Pakistani Christians, meaning 'God's peace with you'.
- From Wales: '**Sut mae**', pronounced 'Shu-my', a greeting from South Wales.
- From north India: '**Sasrikal**', meaning 'welcome'.
- From south India: '**Vanakkam**', meaning 'welcome'.
- From Bangladesh: '**Sharkotom**', Bengali for 'welcome'.
- From Afghanistan: '**Khubistin**', the word for 'welcome' from central Asia.
- From southern Sudan: '**Sene**', pronounced 'sen-ay', part of a greeting from the Zande tribe of southern Sudan.
- From Zambia: '**Gogogoi**'.

I wonder what the various greetings tell us about what is important to people around the world. Ask round your school for more world greetings that you could add to the list and the poster.

World worship: the call to worship

The drum

Activity: Drum beating

You will need a drum from another culture. Your school may have an African Jembe or Indian Tabla drums.

Begin your collective worship or lesson by banging a drum. You could invite some children to come and help. Ask when you might hear drumming. If you were near an African church you might hear drumming like this. In the Western world, Christians usually signal the call to worship with bells; in the Muslim world it is the cry from the **minaret**; but in Africa drumming can be the invitation to worship.

The drum has other purposes, though, apart from making music and being the 'church bell'.

What else might it mean? (Each time this question occurs below, invite others to come and beat the drum.) The drum also calls together the village for a meeting. It gathers the community so that they can discuss, decide and then work together. Christian churches are often banging the drum with this sort of message. They remind us that we need to work together with the Christian family around the world, learning from each other, helping one another and together showing and sharing the love of God.

What else might it mean? It can be a warning of danger. Maybe there are some dangers that we, in the northern part of the world, need to be made aware of by the Christian family elsewhere: dangers of materialism, individualism and global injustice.

What else might it mean? It can be a way to send a message. There are such things as 'talking drums' in Africa whose beats and notes convey a coded message. I wonder what the message is that connects up the global Christian family. What sort of message inspires this family to go on growing? It is the story of Jesus, which Christians are meant to take into all the world.

What else might it mean? This drum is calling people together into a global Christian community of co-workers for God; warning of the dangers of possessions, unfairness and going it alone; gathering people together for worship using the wisdom, inspiration and experiences of the whole worldwide Church and then passing on the message of God's love for all in Jesus.

Activity: Drum prayer

Here is an adapted drum prayer from the Democratic Republic of the Congo. Chant the prayer together to the beat of the drum. Maybe the children can create some more lines.

I'll sing a song of praise to God.
Strike the chords upon the drum.
God who gives us all good things.
Strike the chords upon the drum.
Family, friends and food to eat.
Strike the chords upon the drum.

The light

A service of Christian worship in India looks rather different from church services in the UK. Congregations normally sit on the floor and there will be the smell of incense. The call to worship begins with the lighting of a special lamp, which welcomes the light of Christ into the worship and reminds everyone of God's presence.

Here are some prayers from South India:

As the light is lit, let us pray that the flame of God's living presence may spring up in our hearts and transform us by the knowledge of his glory.

Come, Holy God
Come, loving Source of our life
Come, healing light.

Come, healing Light
Source of our life
Come, healing Light.

Activity: Candle light

Light a candle and invite children to share with each other what it makes them think of. How do they think it might help Christians to get ready for worship?

Here are some reflections about the light of a candle that you could talk about:

- A candle cannot light itself. It needs to receive light from another.
- A candle, when lit, can give away its light without losing the light it has.
- A candle burns as brightly when it is new as when there is only a small amount left.
- A candle's light is sensitive, reacting to the slightest movement of the air around it.
- A candle's light is the same whatever the size, shape or colour of the candle.
- A candle's light is designed to be seen and is best placed high up so that it can give light to all; it is not for hiding away.
- A candle flame burns upward while it sheds its light outward.
- Unless the candle's light is passed on, that light dies when the candle comes to an end.
- At the heart of the candle's light, there is a death happening, as the wick is burnt up and the wax around it melts and evaporates. In the same way, Christians believe that the light of Christ came only from the death of Jesus on the cross.

The picture and the prayer

The liturgy of Orthodox services goes back almost to the beginning of Christian history. They put a special emphasis on the beauty of worship, and this is seen not only in the poetry of Orthodox prayers and in the singing but also in the way that the churches look. They are richly and colourfully decorated and contain many icons. Icons are sacred pictures of Jesus, or scenes from Bible stories or the lives of the saints. Because many people in the past couldn't read, these pictures on the wall or at the altar taught the congregations the important truths of the Christian faith and helped them come close to God.

As part of the call to worship in the Orthodox tradition, candles are lit and a special prayer sung or chanted. In this way, the priest invites God's Holy Spirit to inspire all the worship of the service. If this takes place in a non-church setting, then a special icon will also be placed on a focus table. Pictures of icons can be found on the internet. Perhaps you could choose one that is special to your school in some way.

Activity: Picture prayers

Ask the children what special pictures help them to be still and remember good things, especially when things are hard.

Here is an Orthodox prayer:

O Heavenly King, Comforter, Spirit of Truth;
Present in all places and filling all things;
Treasury of blessings and Giver of life;
Come and dwell in us and cleanse us from every impurity
And, of your goodness, save our souls.

World worship: sharing the Peace

A special feature of Christian worship worldwide is the part of the service known as 'sharing the Peace'.

Jesus' first resurrection greeting to his disciples was 'Peace' (John 20:19). It was only after this that he commissioned them to go out as his representatives and continue his work. In a similar way, when Jesus sent 70 of his followers on their 'Galilee mission', he instructed them first to greet each host with the word 'Peace' (Luke 10:5).

The Christian message to the world is one of peace—peace with God and each other through Jesus Christ. The following activity picks up this idea and uses different words for peace from around the world with accompanying actions that can be used to 'pass the peace'.

Activity: Passing the Peace

Ask your class to stand in a circle. Teach the following 'peace' greetings from around the world and practise them together.

- **Pace** (pronounced 'pach-ay'), from Romania, along with a hug and kisses on each cheek. (You will have to decide how your class will handle this. Maybe 'air kisses' will work.)
- **Shanti**, from India, with hands in a prayer position and a simple bow.
- **Salaam**, from the Middle East, with a bow and one hand on the heart.
- **Wa**, from China, with hands folded across the chest and a deep bow.
- **Amani**, from East Africa, with a hand-thumb-handshake.
- **Mir**, from Russia, with a great bear hug.
- **Peace**, from Great Britain, with a 'normal' handshake.

Send off the different 'peace greetings', one after the other, to the left and the right, leaving a small time gap between each one. Soon everyone should be involved in giving or receiving a peace from around the world, around the circle. There may be some happy confusion! With luck, all the 'peaces' should come back to the leader eventually.

World worship: saying prayers

In Appendix 1 (see page 70), you will find some examples of Christian prayers from around the world that are inspired by different cultural imagery and local concerns. However, even the way that prayers are said in a service will vary greatly from country to country and also within the different traditions.

'All together' prayers

In many Asian countries, notably the very new Christian church in Nepal and the very large church of South Korea, it is the custom for everyone to speak out their prayers at the same time. After all, prayers aren't meant to impress others but are addressed to God, who can hear everyone in the world at the same time. This is also a helpful way to encourage new Christians to start praying, as they don't feel that other members of the congregation are listening to them or judging how well they word their petitions. In the Western tradition, the same prayer is often recited all together, but this is different from individual and different prayers being spoken all at once.

Activity: 'Spoken round' prayer

Start getting the children used to the idea by inviting everyone to say their name and address at the same time. Then move on to naming all the members of their family. Finally, ask everyone to name lots of things they are thankful for or worried about, all at the same time. Children do not have to join in, and, anyway, no one will notice if they do or don't.

Here is a prayer from South Korea that you could use. Divide the class into four groups and ask each group to say a section, all at the same time. Alternatively, start group 1 saying the prayer; then, at the end of the first part, start Group 2, and so on, so that the prayer becomes a 'spoken round'.

Stay with us, God, for the day is far spent and we have not yet recognised your face in each of our sisters and brothers.
Stay with us, God, for the day is far spent and we have not yet shared your bread in grace with our brothers and sisters.
Stay with us, God, for the day is far spent and we have not listened to your word on the lips of our sisters and brothers.
Stay with us, God, because our very night becomes day when you are there.

The special prayer

The one prayer that is used by Christians all around the world is the prayer Jesus taught (Matthew 6:9–13), known as the Lord's Prayer. Often, international gatherings of Christians will use this prayer, each delegate saying it in his or her own language, demonstrating the variety and unity of the Christian family worldwide.

Activity: Lord's Prayer display

Here is a website where you can find the Lord's Prayer in over a thousand languages: www.spiritrestoration.org/Church/lord's-prayer-christus-rex.htm. Choose some countries and print off the prayer to create a display.

Responses

In some Christian traditions, the prayers will be shared between a priest or worship leader, who says some lines, and the members of the congregation, who respond with a short sentence, repeated several times.

One of the most famous prayers used in this way across the world is known as the 'Kyrie Eleison' which is Greek for 'Lord, have mercy'. It is often sung or chanted many times in a service and is a prayer that Christians use to remind themselves that everything they have comes only because of God's love. Bartimaeus, who was blind, made this same simple prayer to Jesus once. You can read his story in Mark 10:46–52.

'Kyrie Eleison', like 'Hallelujah', is one of the most international Christian worship words and is understood the world over. Here it is in some other languages:

- **Swahili**: Bwana na huruma
- **Spanish**: Señor, ten piedad
- **French**: Seigneur, prends pitié
- **Afrikaans**: Here, ontferm
- **Turkish**: Rab merhamet
- **Filipino**: Panginoon maawa
- **Indonesian**: Tuhan kasihanilah

Silence

Perhaps the most universal way of praying, for Christians worldwide, is silent prayer. When Paul gave the Christians in Rome advice on how to pray, he suggested that the deepest prayer is that which is too deep for words (Romans 8:26). It is then that God's Holy Spirit helps Christians to pray most effectively. However, silence isn't easy, so different cultures use a variety of local symbols to help them focus their silent prayer.

In the **catacombs** of Rome where the first Christians hid from persecution, simple pictures of fish or an anchor, drawn on the walls, helped them pray. A piece of art or an icon can also be a doorway into prayer. Sometimes a special stone or a religious souvenir or relic can help. Many traditions use the smell of incense.

Here is a prayer from Sri Lanka that suggests another useful local symbol:

Even as the water falls on dry tea leaves
and brings out their flavour,
So may your Spirit fall on us and renew us
So that we may bring refreshment
and joy to others.

Activity: Silent prayer

Show the class some special icons or pictures from other cultures. What do they think about these images? Explore with the class what would help them to pray silently.

Physical prayer

Christians around the world vary greatly in how and when they pray.

Orthodox worshippers in Eastern Europe, the Middle East, Egypt and Ethiopia stand when they pray. In fact, they stand for most of their long but colourful church services.

Christian worshippers in India and Pakistan will usually sit crosslegged on the floor in a position that Westerners would describe as yoga-like and suited to meditation.

In some Christian traditions, worshippers will even prostrate themselves on the ground, making the sign of the cross over every part of their body—eyes, face, heart and their whole person, from their feet to their head and across themselves.

Catholic Christians will bow the knee before the altar (**genuflect**) and also cross themselves whenever the name of Jesus is mentioned in prayer. Catholics make the horizontal part of the sign of the cross from their left to the right, whereas Orthodox Christians move their hands right to left.

Many Christians from all parts of the globe prefer to kneel when they pray.

The **monastic** tradition of Europe established a pattern of regular prayers seven times a day.

There is also a great variety in the way hands are held in prayer. Christians of the Pentecostal tradition usually pray with one or both hands held aloft. Other

Christians hold out cupped hands as if ready to receive, and there are those who either fold hands or place their palms side by side, with fingers pointing upward.

Orthodox Christians use knotted prayer ropes to help them pray important repeated prayers. Catholic Christians use rosary beads for the same purpose.

Activity: Prayer positions

You can read what Jesus said about prayer in Matthew 6:5–8; Luke 11:5–13 and Luke 18:1–8. What are his guidelines for Christian prayer? Ask the children what positions they would recommend for prayer, and why.

There is an RE lesson outline about prayer, with further useful links, at www.barnabasinschools.org.uk/2720.

Chapter 6

Everywhere a sign

Overview of content

For Christians all over the world, the **sacraments** of baptism and Communion (the **Mass**) are two key elements of their worship of God. Baptism marks the moment of decision to follow Jesus Christ. Communion is the one service that Jesus left his followers as a way of remembering him and receiving the grace they need to go on believing in him. Through the use of water, bread and wine, Christians encourage each other in their faith. Around the world, different approaches to these sacraments give insights into why they are so special to Christian believers. This chapter explores what these two services look like in a variety of countries, with activity suggestions for the classroom and ideas to develop in collective worship.

World worship: Baptism

Baptism is one of the key Christian services, practised by almost all Christian traditions around the world. Only the Quakers and the Salvation Army have no baptism service. It is the service of welcome into the Christian faith and is called a sacrament, which means that ordinary earthly elements (in this case, water, candlelight and oil) are used in a service to symbolise an extraordinary connection with God.

Some Christians baptise (or **christen**) babies, believing that they are welcomed into the family of the faith at birth, and remain under the prayerful guidance of parents and sponsors (**godparents**) until such time as they can decide for themselves to follow the way of Jesus. Other traditions prefer to baptise people when they are older or as adults, when they can speak up and own for themselves what they are doing. There is variety, too, in whether baptism candidates experience a full immersion in the water or merely a sprinkling. Some of these differences stem from practicalities such as climate and the availability of water, but it could be said that a full immersion is more properly symbolic of a new start in life—being raised, as it were, from a 'death' of drowning (see Romans 6:3–5).

In many countries, those being baptised:

- wear white.
- are anointed with oil, which is symbolic of the Holy Spirit.
- are invisibly marked with the sign of the cross with water on their forehead to link them to the death and resurrection of Jesus.
- are given a lighted candle to remind them of their new life as God's followers, called to pass on the light of God in this world.

Eastern Orthodox Christians usually insist on a complete threefold immersion. In fact, everything is done in threes, in the name of the Father, Son and Holy Spirit. In the Ethiopian Orthodox Church, the priest also walks around the child or adult three times with an open Bible.

Where candidates are sprinkled, the water is kept in a special container called a font and is blessed with a prayer before the baptism. Traditionally, fonts are eight-sided, because it was on the eighth day (counting from Palm Sunday) that Jesus rose from the dead, and they are situated near the entrance to a church because baptism is the Christian's way into the faith.

Full-immersion (or submersion) baptism is the most common practice in many African and African-American Christian congregations.

> The Church of England introduces the meaning of baptism on its website in this way:
>
> In baptism, you as parents are: thanking God for his gift of life, making a decision to start your child on the journey of faith and asking for the Church's support. For your child, baptism marks the start of a journey of faith, which involves turning away from all that is evil, turning towards Christ and becoming a member of the local and worldwide Christian family.

One feature of baptisms in other cultures, particularly where community or tribal life is strong, is that of group or family baptism. This was practised in the New Testament, too, and was also widespread during the first millennium of the Christian Church, when the baptism of a king would mean that the whole of his court and family received baptism at the same time. It is less common today.

The words of decision and the promises made are very important in baptism, whether made by an adult or by a sponsor on behalf of a baby. In the Coptic Orthodox Church in Egypt, candidates face the west when they renounce the devil, as the setting sun is seen as the place of an ending, and they face east when they make their promises to turn to Christ—east being the place of sunrise and a new beginning. The candidates also wear special crowns as symbols of their new status as members of Christ's royal family.

Epiphany (6 January) is the feast of the Baptism of Christ in the Orthodox tradition. You can read what happened in Matthew 3:13–17. This service is celebrated with great ceremony in the Orthodox Church and particularly in Ethiopia, where the priests stand beneath huge decorated umbrellas in their colourful robes. Christ's baptism is believed to be a baptism on behalf of the whole world, and it ushers in a new beginning for creation after the brokenness and falling away from God that happened in the garden of Eden. Because Jesus touches the water, everything can be renewed.

Activity: Baptism stories

Share stories of baptisms and christenings that children in the class have seen. Which parts of the service seemed to be the most important? Discuss whether the children think it would be better for people to wait until they are older to be baptised. Which baptism traditions from the worldwide Church described above do they find most attractive?

You can watch an Ethiopian baptism online at www.youtube.com/watch?v=6NvrA7tFIQg

World worship: Communion

Communion—or the **Mass** or **Eucharist**, as it is also known—is the most important service for most Christians the world over. It is based on the words and actions of Jesus during his last supper, the night before he was crucified. You can read about it in Luke 22:14–23.

The simple act of breaking bread and drinking wine was the way Jesus asked his followers to remember him. It was meant to help them understand what he was going to do on the cross for the whole world. It is also, like baptism, a sacrament, when ordinary earthly elements (in this case, bread and wine) are used in a service to symbolise an extraordinary connection with God.

However, in many places of the world, bread and wine do not properly represent the chief food and drink of the believers' culture, so Christians in some countries use local alternatives:

- In many Pacific regions, the coconut is a country's most useful food, providing almost everything they need for living. Therefore, it can truly represent Jesus in Communion in the same symbolic way that bread and wine do.
- Indonesian Christians use lime juice and cassava for the same reasons.
- In Central Mexico, some indigenous churches use tortillas for bread and either a corn drink called pozol or coffee for the wine.
- In areas where rice is the staple diet, rice cakes and rice wine are sometimes used.
- In sub-Saharan Africa, the banana tree is the equivalent source of much that sustains life.

Here is an extract from a letter from missionaries working in Uganda that illustrates the use of bananas in this way.

Riddle: What is green or red or brown or yellow? It can be as small as your finger, as long as your foot and grows in hands.

Solution: A banana.

If you like bananas, then Uganda is a good place to live. They grow everywhere, and not just the large yellow type you see in the UK. Bananas are used in all sorts of ways.

They can, of course, be eaten as they are. Some prefer the small, fat and pale yellow ones but others are large, red and brown as well as yellow.

There are also the green matoke bananas, which are hard. They are peeled like potatoes and steamed, wrapped in banana leaves. Most Ugandans can't go many days without having matoke for dinner. The fruit may also turn up as banana cake or chewy banana pancakes.

You can also drink banana! Mashing up banana with lots of sugar makes a popular syrupy drink. If left for a while, this becomes banana wine, which is even used at Communion in church.

If you lose the top of a container, a banana makes a very effective stopper.

The leaf of the banana plant is also extremely versatile. It can be quickly broken off when it rains, to serve as an instant umbrella. It can be used as a plate, a mat or a food wrapper.

It provides a shady cover when placed over young seedlings, small animals or people, of course.

The trunk of the banana plant is made up of a supple, woody fibre which is good for making mats and string.

Banana leaves rolled and tied together can produce a very good football.

There are banana plantations in Uganda and, indeed, most homes will have the plants growing in the garden. With all this background, it is interesting to look at Jesus' words in John 6:35. Since bananas are far more important and commonplace a commodity than bread in Uganda, it seems much more appropriate to a Ugandan Christian to think of Jesus as 'the banana of life'.

In the Christian churches that do use bread, there are often elaborate rituals for its preparation. Greek Orthodox Christians stamp their special round Communion bread (called *Prosphora*) with the initials ICXC NIKA, which means 'Christ conquers'. The following 'bread of life' prayer is also said over the dough before it is baked:

O Lord Jesus Christ, only begotten Son of the eternal Father, who said, 'Without me you can do nothing.' O Lord, my God, with faith I accept these words. Help me, a sinner, to prepare the bread of the offering, that the works of my hands may be acceptable at the holy table and may become, through the work of the Holy Spirit, the communion of your most pure body for me and all your people. In the name of the Father and of the Son and the Holy Spirit. Amen

In a similar way, the Orthodox Church in Romania divides up the round loaf into sections that represent the angels and archangels of heaven, the people who have already died and gone to be with God, and the present congregation of those still on earth. The Communion bread therefore reminds believers that they are part of a huge family that stretches across time and space.

Activity: Communion breads

Use the internet to find out what sort of breads might be used for Communion in different parts of the world —for example, chapatis in India and kisera bread in Sudan.

Discuss with the class what alternatives to bread and wine might be more appropriate for some culture groups in our own society. How would they help people to understand the Christian message better?

Debate with your class whether continuing to use bread and wine is better or worse than using alternatives.

Chapter 7

Everywhere a feast

Overview of content

Harvest thanksgiving, Christmas and Easter are three of the major Christian festivals over the course of a year. (A fourth, Pentecost, is covered in Chapter 3.) This chapter explores some of the many ways in which each festival is marked and celebrated across the world. With each section there are also suggestions for classroom activities and ideas that can be developed in collective worship.

World worship: celebrating harvest

A successful harvest is important for most communities, especially those people in the majority world who are totally dependent on growing crops and keeping livestock for their food. Drought or flooding can mean the difference between life and death, so Christians in all places have always devised services of prayer and thanksgiving linked to harvest. In the New Testament we read how Christians in one part of the world sent financial help to their brothers and sisters elsewhere who were experiencing a bad harvest (see Acts 11:27–29).

This care, across cultures and continents, is something that Christian aid and relief agencies still facilitate today. Four of the major agencies are listed below, and you can read more about their work on their websites. Many of these organisations also provide resources for school lessons and assemblies, especially at harvest time.

- CAFOD: www.cafod.org.uk
- Christian Aid: www.christianaid.org.uk
- Oxfam: www.oxfam.org.uk
- TearFund: www.tearfund.org

Each of the three pilgrim festivals of the Jewish faith—Passover, Pentecost and Tabernacles—has an association with harvest. At Passover, the first offering of the year's harvest was presented at the temple as a sheaf of barley. Pentecost (or *Shavuot*) marked the harvesting of the grain, and Tabernacles came at the completion of that harvest, when the people of God made temporary shelters outdoors (*sukkahs*) to remind them of their time in the desert.

These three festivals also speak of God's covenant love to his people, as they are linked to the story of the great rescue from slavery in Egypt, the giving of the law at Sinai and God's provision for his people on their way to the promised land.

Harvest can also carry these connections for Christians as they remember Jesus Christ (who is described as a Passover lamb), the gift of the Holy Spirit (who writes God's laws on their hearts) and the sheltering presence of God, who promises to be with them on their journey of faith. So, for Christians everywhere, harvest festival services are not only an opportunity to be thankful for the fruit of the earth but also a time to celebrate the character of God.

In some Christian churches around the world, every Sunday service can seem like a harvest thanksgiving: rather than having a plate passed round to collect money (which is often in short supply), chickens in cages, fruit in baskets and home-made foodstuffs are brought up to the front, blessed and taken out into the local community to be redistributed to people in need.

Activity: Trees of life

Different trees are important to various communities around the world. Use the internet to research the following trees and their significance to sustaining life in the associated countries.

- The banana tree of East Africa
- The palm tree of the Middle East
- The coconut tree of the Pacific Islands
- The baobab tree of central and southern Africa
- The bamboo tree of China
- The rubber tree of Latin America
- The moringa tree of Asia

Link the importance of these trees to the tree of life described in the opening and closing chapters of the Bible (Genesis 2:9 and Revelation 22:2).

Activity: Wells and water

Make water the focus for your harvest exploration and talk about:

- The joy of rainfall
- The importance of wells
- The disaster of drought
- The devastation of flooding
- The dangers of dirty water
- The uses of clean water

Link this to stories of wells and water from the Bible. For example, find out what happened to the following Old Testament people when they visited wells: Abraham's servant (Genesis 24); Isaac (Genesis 26:17–33); Jacob (Genesis 29:1–14); Joseph (Genesis 37:12–28); Moses (Exodus 2:15–20). Look at the special kind of water that Jesus talked about in John 4:13–15 and 7:37–39.

****

In many African languages, the word for 'rain' is closely linked to the word for 'God' or 'life'. In one region of Kenya, the word for 'rain' is the same as the word for 'fatness'. Here is a prayer of the Suk people from East Africa:

God, give us fatness and we, thy people,
shall be well.
We shall be well and healthy; and that is sweet.
Amen

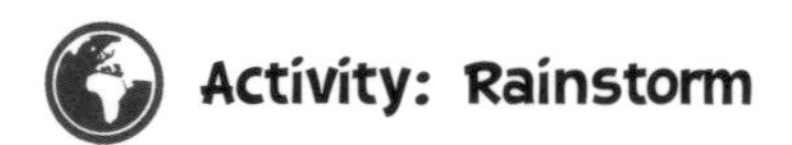

Activity: Rainstorm

Here is a very simple idea to involve a class or whole assembly in making a 'rainstorm' together. Invite everyone to tap on the palm of one hand, first with one finger, then two, then three, and so on. By controlling the build-up of sound, you can create what is heard from the fall of the first few raindrops to the roar of a tropical downpour.

Activity: Harvest colours

Use colours to explore the positive and negative meanings of harvest for Christians around the world:

- **Black**: a seed of hope but also the burned tree stumps from deforestation.
- **Red**: shiny ripened fruit but also the colour of debts that are impossible to pay back.
- **Yellow**: crops ready to harvest but also the colour of human skin poisoned by exposure to pesticides.
- **Green**: bright leaves of healthy trees but also the colour of mould on vegetables that can't be sold because they are not good enough for Western supermarkets.
- **Orange**: juicy fruit but also the sandy colour of areas turned into desert in a drought.
- **White**: blossom that carries the hope of fruitfulness but also the colour of mildew when fruit is diseased.
- **Brown**: good fertile soil but also the dirty water of a flood.
- **Blue**: clear healthy water but also the colour of cloudless skies when the rains don't come.

Link the colours with the story of Noah and the rainbow from Genesis 9.

Activity: Global awareness

Nowadays we are deeply aware that everything that happens globally is linked together. Poor harvests in one place will mean higher prices for goods elsewhere. Unfair trade rules followed by one part of the world mean poverty for innocent sufferers in another. Each of us is a world citizen.

You could say that our generic e-mail address ought to be me@theworld.com. But what might the 'com' stand for? Talk through the following possible answers with a class:

- me@theworld.complacent
- me@theworld.comfortable
- me@theworld.compassionate
- me@theworld.community-minded
- me@theworld.committed

*****

In southern India, harvest festival is called 'Pongal' and covers a three-day period starting on 15 January. It is also the time for a grand spring-clean. People buy new clothes and even new pots and pans for the kitchen. Outside the home, the family create special 'rangoli' patterns in coloured powders on the ground. Popular designs include the lotus flower and the shape of the mango leaf.

Pongal means 'boiled up', and the festival meal is raw rice boiled into a hard lump and served with many kinds of vegetables. Most people in Tamil Nadu are vegetarian.

Day 2 of the festival is known as 'Cow Pongal'. Cows are given a day off from ploughing. They are bathed and decorated with flower garlands, and even have their horns painted. This is a way for the people to express thanks for God's creation of the animals, which help them in their everyday lives.

Day 3 is especially for the children. They receive presents, and special poems that they have written are broadcast over loudspeakers. They eat sugar cane sweets cut straight from the tall, thick cane stems. They are very chewy and the fibrous parts are spat out, not swallowed. The cows enjoy their own sweets in the form of the green leaves from the tops of the stems.

Christians sometimes whitewash their homes at harvest and add their own decorations in the shape of large three-dimensional stars made from coloured paper or cardboard. The stars are punched with small holes and used as lampshades, with lights placed inside. This reminds Christians of their belief that Jesus is the light of the world.

A template for a festival star can be found at www.barnabasinchurches.org.uk/make-an-indian-christmas-star/

Activity: Rangoli

You could make your own rangoli pattern. Using glue, trace thin decorative lines on card in a pattern of your choosing. Sprinkle different coloured glitter on to the card, wait for some of the glitter to stick, dust off the excess and continue with more of the design. Be imaginative and colourful.

****

Other harvest ideas can be found on the Barnabas websites. Visit www.barnabasinschools.org.uk and www.barnabasinchurches.org.uk and search for 'harvest'.

World church harvest prayers and poems

This African poem celebrates harvest and all things African.

All you big things, bless the Lord.
Mount Kilimanjaro and Lake Victoria,
The Rift Valley and the Serengeti Plain,
Fat baobabs and shady mango trees,
All eucalyptus and tamarind trees,
Bless the Lord.
Praise and extol him for ever and ever.

All you tiny things, bless the Lord.
Busy black ants and hopping fleas,
Wriggling tadpoles and mosquito larvae,
Flying locusts and water drops,
Pollen dust and tsetse flies,
Millet seeds and dried dagaa,
Bless the Lord.
Praise and extol him for ever and ever.

Here are some harvest prayers.

Lord, sweeten the waters.
Lord, sweeten the grass.
Lord, sweeten and swell all the rivers.
Lord, thicken all forests.
Lord, sweeten all animals.

Lord, give us land.
Lord, let the land be green.
Lord, give us rains.
Lord, give us fruitful lands.
Lord, sweeten all rivers.

A MAASAI PRAYER FROM KENYA

Glory to God for his good things
Glory to God for his blessings
Glory to God who has sustained us with gifts
Glory to God who has nourished us
Glory to God who has satisfied us
Glory to God by whose will we are alive
Glory to God who is merciful
May his mercies be upon us by the prayers
of the mother of God,
Mary, and all the saints for ever and ever.
Amen

A PRAYER FROM THE SYRIAN ORTHODOX CHURCH

World worship: Christmas

Christmas is celebrated by Christians the world over. This is the time when they remember that God came to earth and was born as a baby. The belief that God actually became a human being and shared in life on earth is central to the Christian faith and is known as the **incarnation**. You can read the story in Luke 2:1–21.

The four-week build-up to Christmas is also very important and is called Advent. It is the time when services and special Bible readings from the Old Testament help Christians get ready for the story of this unique birth.

Activity: Advent biscuits

Why not make some special Ethiopian Advent biscuits? These are called *Dabo Kolo* (literally 'bread nibbles').

You will need:

- 650g plain flour
- 3 tablespoons of sugar
- a pinch of salt
- 225ml water
- 4 tablespoons of oil

Mix the flour, sugar and salt together. Add water, a little at a time, and mix well. Add the oil and knead to make a stiff dough. Roll into long, thin rolls, no more than 1cm in diameter. With scissors, cut shapes no more than 1cm wide, turning the roll every time you cut, to get different shapes. Bake on a tray for 5–10 minutes at 150°C until light brown, moving the shapes around now and again.

For variety, you could add cinnamon, use less sugar and add paprika to make a savoury version, or add vegetable colourings.

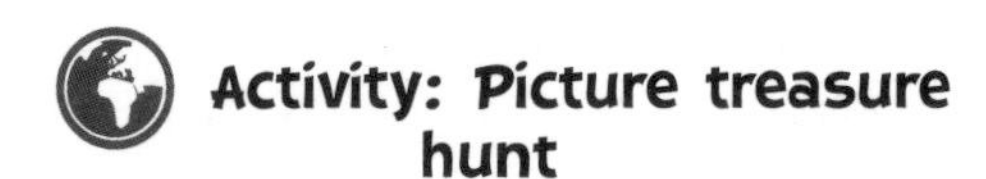

Activity: Picture treasure hunt

Collect sets of clip-art images relating to Christmas from around the world. Include a star; a poinsettia; a camel; a crib scene; an Advent wreath; a candle; an angel; shoes (left out for presents in central Europe on 6 December, St Nicholas' day); holly; a Christmas cactus; mistletoe; bells; a Christmas rose; a Christmas tree; a stocking.

Hide the images around the classroom or school and have a 'Christmas treasure hunt', challenging the children individually or in small groups to collect a full set of pictures. Use them as a discussion starter about the wide range of symbols used in Christmas celebrations.

You could hang the images on to a **Jesse tree**, alongside other symbols that will act as reminders of the Bible stories that lead up to Christmas. There are instructions about making a Jesse tree in various books and also on the internet.

*****

In Mexico during Advent, Christian families dress up as Mary and Joseph and visit neighbours, asking for a room and telling them why the birth of Jesus is so important. This tradition is called '**posada**' (which means 'inn': see Luke 2:7) and has been adopted in other countries in recent years. Nativity sets of Joseph and Mary travel on a rota basis, visiting a different family or place every night. The night when Mary and Joseph 'stay' provides a great opportunity to invite guests around to share the true meaning of Christmas with a prayer evening or the singing of Christmas carols.

Activity: Posada

Why not send a simple nativity set round the homes of children in the class, inviting each home to add a small simple decoration or animal? The set could become the centrepiece of a Christmas service at the end of the term.

*****

In South India, people get up very early in the morning on Christmas Day and put on their best clothes for a church service that starts at 6.00am. The women and girls wear sweet-smelling jasmine flowers in their hair. The service ends at dawn, with the sunrise reminding everyone that Jesus, the light of the world, has been born.

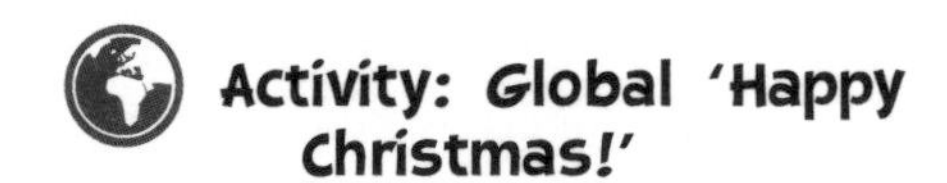

Activity: Global 'Happy Christmas!'

Learn how to say 'Happy Christmas' in various languages. Here are some to start you off.

- **Albanian**: Gezur Krislinjden
- **Arabic**: Idah Saidan Wa Sanah Jadidah
- **Bengali**: Shuvo Naba Barsha
- **Bohemian**: Vesele Vanoce
- **Brazilian**: Boas Festas e Feliz Ano Novo
- **Chinese (Mandarin)**: Kung His Hsin Nien bing Chu Shen Tan
- **Dutch (The Netherlands)**: Prettig Kerstfeest
- **Eskimo (Inupik)**: Jutdlime pivdluarit ukiortame pivdluaritlo!
- **Esperanto**: Gajan Kristnaskon
- **Finnish**: Hyvaa joulua
- **French**: Joyeux Noël
- **Gaelic (Irish)**: Nolag mhaith Dhuit Agus Bliain Nua Fe Mhaise
- **Gaelic (Scots)**: Nollaig chridheil agus Bliadhna mhath ùr!
- **German**: Fröhliche Weihnachten
- **Greek**: Kala Christouyenna!
- **Hausa**: Barka da Kirsimatikuma Barka da Sabuwar Shekara!
- **Hindi**: Shub Naya Baras
- **Indonesian**: Selamat Hari Natal

- **Iraqi**: Idah Saidan Wa Sanah Jadidah
- **Italian**: Buone Feste Natalizie
- **Japanese**: Shinnen omedeto. Kurisumasu Omedeto
- **Korean**: Sung Tan Chuk Ha
- **Maori**: Meri Kirihimete
- **Norwegian**: God Jul, *or* Gledelig Jul
- **Philippines**: Maligayan Pasko!
- **Portuguese**: Feliz Natal
- **Singhalese**: Subha nath thalak Vewa. Subha Aluth Awrudhak Vewa
- **Spanish**: Feliz Navidad
- **Swedish**: God Jul, *or* Ett Gott Nytt År
- **Tagalog**: Maligayamg Pasko. Masaganang Bagong Taon
- **Ukrainian**: Srozhdestvom Kristovym
- **Urdu**: Naya Saal Mubarak Ho
- **Welsh**: Nadolig Llawen
- **Yoruba**: E ku odun, e ku iye'dun!

*****

In the following letter, a Christian in Pakistan writes to friends in the UK about the way the festival is celebrated in her country.

I expect you will all be having a lovely Christmas with lots of presents, tasty food and colourful decorations in your homes. The special thing about Christmas for the Christian children in Pakistan is that they all get a new set of clothes. They may sometimes get presents too, if the family has enough money, but whatever their circumstances, parents do try to give their children something new to wear. Most people do not have Christmas trees in their houses, but they do decorate their homes and the churches with coloured streamers and tinsel. There are competitions for singing Christmas carols and for reciting verses from the Bible which the children have learned off by heart. There are some Bible quizzes for young people and nativity plays or Christmas dramas. On Christmas Eve, everyone visits their neighbours with trays of fruit and nuts and sweets to share.

25 December is a holiday for everyone in Pakistan, not just for the Christians, because it is also the birthday of a man called Mohammed Ali Jinnah. When India was about to become an independent country in 1947, Mr Jinnah said that the Muslims of India should have a country of their own, separate from the Hindus. As a result, part of India became Pakistan, where most of the population are Muslims. Mr Jinnah died in 1948 but he is remembered today and is called 'Father of the Nation'.

Activity: Paper decorations

There are a number of paper craft ideas for making special decorations associated with Christmas in different countries, including sunburst designs from Sweden, *Weihnacht* angels from Germany, Kalanda stars from Greece, interlocking bells and woven hearts as tree decorations from Germany and Denmark, Santa Lucia hats from Sweden (for 13 December), Piñata for posada parties in Mexico and a Farol star from Spain. Instructions can be found on the internet or in books such as *Papercrafts Around the World* by Phyllis and Noel Fiarotta (Sterling Juvenile, 2000).

*****

In the following piece, a Western Christian writes about her first Christmas in South Korea.

Christmas really only started yesterday (Christmas Eve) with morning service at the Hang Dong Anglican Church, and it felt quite refreshing to start singing the traditional carols then, for the first time, rather than having already sung them for weeks beforehand. The Koreans mostly use the traditional 'western' carol tunes, although the choir did sing some Korean items too. Then there was the traditional noodle lunch. At 7.30pm there was a baptism service (five adults and a baby)—traditional on Christmas Eve—followed by another meal together. After that we all gathered to hear the children sing and perform and then family groups sang songs and carols, followed by most people in the church getting up and singing in pairs or groups. I think that would be unusual in the UK! I felt involved too, as I had been asked to play my flute. At 12.00 midnight we had the Christmas Communion. The whole day had felt very good to me.

Activity: Christmas songs

Introduce some Christmas-related songs from other cultures, such as 'He came down' from the Cameroon (see *Many and Great: Songs of the world church*, Wild Goose) and 'Jesous Ahatonhia' from Canada (see *Sent by the Lord: Songs of the world church*, also Wild Goose).

 Activity: Christmas stories

Read together a story from another part of the world that is told at Christmas time. See, for example, *Joy to the world: Christmas stories from around the globe* by Saviour Pirotta (Frances Lincoln, 2010).

*****

In Kenya, passion flower leaves and fresh flowers decorate the church at Christmas. It is also a time for the renewal of promises. The baby in a Kenyan nativity play is laid in a locally made basket called a Kionda. This represents the manger in the Christmas story. The wise men who visit are often represented by people from different local tribes (for example, one Bantu, one Nyamwezi and one Kikuyu) and they bring gifts such as beads, skins and ivory.

 Activity: Wise men and gifts

Decide which three different groups of people might represent the wise men in your community. What gifts might they bring?

 Activity: Tangram pictures

Using the seven shapes that make up the Chinese puzzle of the Tangram (search online for illustrations of this puzzle), challenge groups to create various characters and symbols from the Christmas story, such as a camel, a manger, Mary kneeling and a star.

*****

Any of the activities in this section could be introduced during the weeks leading up to Christmas and included as part of a class presentation or end-of-term assembly.

Useful resources

- There are many websites dedicated to Christmas customs around the world. For example, see www.woodlands-junior.kent.sch.uk/teacher/christmas.html. Ask some groups to do some research of their own and report back to the others.
- See www.barnabasinchurches.org.uk/joy-to-the-world/ for ideas of how to celebrate Christmas with symbols, songs, greetings and activities from around the world.
- A very useful pack of resources for celebrating a global Christmas is *Born Among Us* (from the Methodist Church), an all-age Christmas resource inspired by the world church, containing pictures, music and activity sheets. Though no longer available new, many Educational Resource Centres will have a copy of this pack.
- Out of the Ark Music has a special global Christmas musical for schools: see www.outoftheark.co.uk/products/nativities/children-of-the-world.html

World worship: celebrating Easter

Holy Week and Easter Day are the most important celebrations for Christians around the world. The story of Jesus' last days in Jerusalem, his death on a cross and his coming back to life are at the heart of what Christians believe. The story is recorded in each of the New Testament Gospels and summarised by Paul in 1 Corinthians 15:1–8. Paul goes on to say that the resurrection is the most important part of the Christian faith and that everything depends on it being true.

Easter is sometimes called the Feast of Feasts, and most churches have a large range of worship services at this time of year (in March or April). The drama of the story is re-enacted in the church traditions for Palm Sunday and Good Friday. In many countries, there are street processions or services that move from station to station around a church as Christians remember the journey of Jesus to the cross.

Easter Sunday is the climax of the story and, in many Christian traditions, the service takes place at midnight or just before dawn. The church begins in darkness, but, to represent the rising of Jesus from the dead, the special Easter candle (the **Paschal** candle) is lit. From that flame, worshippers light other candles to fill the church with light. This is a way to remember that Jesus' death and resurrection have brought new light to the world.

*****

Easter is a very special time in the Romanian Orthodox Church. The main three days of the Easter celebration are Good Friday, Great and Holy Saturday and Easter Day.

- Good Friday is a **fast** day (when food is not eaten). There is a special service to mark the hours when Jesus hung on the cross.
- On Great and Holy Saturday, the church remembers how Jesus descended into hell and released the people who had been trapped there until his death. The service re-enacts Jesus calling Adam out of hell, followed by the other great

biblical heroes. In Romanian homes, bread is baked and taken to the church to be blessed. It is eaten later by the family.

- Easter Day begins in darkness very early on Sunday morning. Only the Paschal candle is alight. The congregation and the priest act out, through readings, the drama of the women coming to the tomb to find the body of Jesus. The question is asked: 'Whom do you seek?' followed by 'Why do you seek for the living among the dead? He is not here. He is risen.' The congregation then replies in a great Easter shout, 'He is risen indeed. Hallelujah!'

Activity: Easter acclamation

On Easter morning, Christian congregations in many lands and in many languages repeat the same great 'Easter acclamation' or shout of praise: 'Christ is risen. He is risen indeed!' As a way of sharing in this proclamation of the central truth of the Christian faith, why not teach and use versions of this shout in other languages?

- Christos a inviat. Adverat a inviat (Romanian)
- Christos anestee. Aleethos anestee (Greek)
- Al Masih Quaam. Quaam Hallelujah (Arabic)
- Christos Vos Kres. Voistin Vos Kres (Russian)
- Yesu Azali Na Bomoi. Hallelujah, Yesu Azali Na Bomoi (from the Democratic Republic of the Congo)

*****

Another strong Orthodox tradition is the painting of Easter eggs with symbols of the resurrection and new life. Ukraine is one of the countries of Eastern Europe that has most faithfully preserved the art of painting eggs as special gifts for Easter. The tradition is called 'Pysanky' and a range of recognised patterns are used.

Activity: Egg painting

Painting eggs requires careful preparation. Either remove the insides of an egg by blowing it through a small hole at each end (it is possible to buy a special tool to do this from craft shops) or hardboil an egg and allow it to cool. (Remember that if you paint a hardboiled egg, the insides will eventually go bad.)

To colour the egg, boil it for about an hour in hot water with a dye added.

You could use natural dyes. For example:

- **Red:** use the skins from red onions.
- **Pink:** soak the eggs in cranberry juice.
- **Yellow:** to a cup of hot water add one to one-and-a-half teaspoons of turmeric.
- **Golden tan:** use the skins from yellow onions.
- **Brown:** to a cup of hot water add one tablespoon of instant coffee and half a tablespoon of vinegar.

Allow the egg to dry and/or cool. Then, using a small vice or makeshift clamp to keep the egg in place, paint on patterns using a thin paint brush and acrylic paints. Allow the paint to dry and then varnish the egg to protect the pattern.

Basic patterns include coloured parallel lines around the egg near the top and bottom, within which are zigzag marks or dots; flower petals and long green leaves; occasional cross shapes.

*****

Lent and Easter are full of special traditions in the Ukraine. There, the Sunday before Easter is called Willow Sunday. Willow branches are waved instead of the palm leaves used in Western churches.

In Ukrainian homes the Easter basket is the pride and joy of most families. It is put together with great care, following strict guidelines. This wicker basket is taken to the Sunday morning service at Easter and is blessed before the contents are shared with the family at an Easter breakfast meal. The basket contains a newly embroidered serviette or white napkin, on which is laid a sample of the foods that a household can now eat at Easter, following the Lenten fast:

- Paska (special Easter bread, decorated with traditional patterns); usually a candle is placed at the centre, which will be lit during the church service
- Dyed eggs in a variety of colours, but especially red
- Salt
- Butter in decorative shapes
- Cheese
- A small ring of sausage

After the Easter Day service and the great shout that 'Christ is risen' (*Christos Voskres*), there is the sharing of the Paska bread and special dances (*Habilky*).

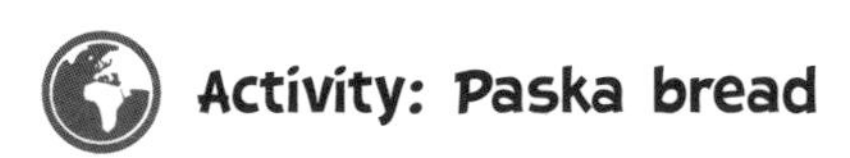

Activity: Paska bread

Prepare some dough for the special Paska bread. Roll some additional dough into cubes and then twist and bend them to make the traditional decorative shapes (sun motifs, square crosses, scrolls, braids, rosettes and birds).

To make Paska, mix together 50g yeast, 1 tablespoon of milk, 1 tablespoon of sugar and 2–3 tablespoons of water. Dissolve the yeast, wait until the mixture bubbles and then add 400g flour and 400ml warm milk.

Allow the dough to rise. Then add 800g flour, 3 whole eggs, 3 egg yolks, 125g sugar, a quarter tablespoon of salt, one rind of a lemon, the juice of an orange and 125g melted butter.

Knead the mixture well, until the dough is elastic. Add the decorations and bake for 15–20 minutes at 220°C/Gas Mark 6.

*****

In Sri Lanka, Christian churches are very busy as Easter approaches. Costumes are made for special Easter plays. Instead of simply being read from the Gospels, the story is told in speeches, music (mainly using drums), songs, dance and drama. These performances are in the open air and are very colourful and well attended. Different ways are explored to present the events surrounding the death and resurrection of Jesus.

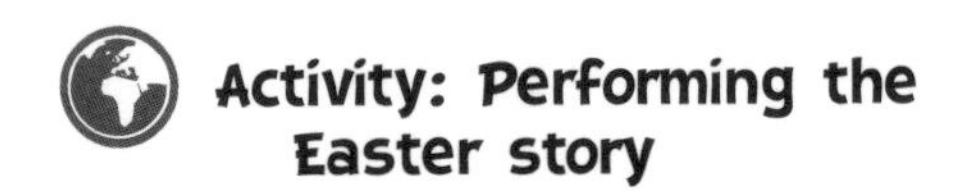

Activity: Performing the Easter story

As a group or a class, you could try to imitate the Christians of Sri Lanka, using some of their ideas to tell your own version of the Easter story. For example:

- Use drums to beat out rhythms expressing the sadness of Jesus on the way to the cross and his dying.
- Dance to celebrate the surprise and joy of the resurrection day.
- Write poems or short speeches to describe the time Jesus prayed in Gethsemane and when the disciples fell asleep.
- Mime how Jesus was tried unfairly and then rejected by the crowd.
- Use Sri Lankan images, such as lotus flower patterns, to illustrate a picture of Mary meeting Jesus in the garden.

*****

In Tahiti, a coconut is marked with a cross, then kicked, rolled and finally hacked with a knife as a moving commentary on the events of Good Friday. The service concludes with the water and meat of the coconut being used to celebrate Communion.

*****

A story about bamboo is told in China to help Christians understand the truth of the Easter story.

The bamboo tree stood tall and straight, holding up its head proudly because it knew it was the master's favourite plant. Its tall, straight stems, with their thick bunches of waving leaves, were far taller than he was. When its master walked in the garden, the bamboo tree would bow its proud head in greeting.

One day, the master stood before the bamboo tree and said, 'Bamboo, bamboo, I am going to cut you down.'

'Cut me down! Oh no, master, no!'

'Yes. You cannot serve me unless you let me cut you down.'

The bamboo tree bowed its head sadly. 'Very well, master. Cut me down if that is the only way I can serve you.'

'It *is* the only way,' said the master. So he cut the bamboo tree down.

The next day, the master stood looking at the proud bamboo lying on the ground, its stems long and straight and its leaves spread out.

'Bamboo, bamboo,' said the master, 'I must cut off your leaves, all of them.'

'Very well,' said the bamboo. 'Cut off all my leaves if that is the only way I can serve you.'

The bamboo tree lay alone for a time, thinking sadly of all its lost beauty and wondering what else the master had in store for it. Presently, the master returned and said, 'Bamboo, bamboo, you are fine and strong and straight. I shall split you in half from top to bottom and take out your core.'

'Oh no, master, no,' cried the bamboo tree. 'I shall die if you do that. I will serve you any way I can, but do not split me in two.'

'Bamboo, bamboo, you cannot serve me unless I split you in two and take out your core.'

'As you will, master,' whispered the bamboo tree. So the master split the bamboo tree from end to end and took out the core. Then he laid the two halves of the stem end to end and fastened them firmly together. One end he laid to the mouth of a little spring of water which bubbled out of the ground and lost itself among the mosses and stones. The other end he placed in his rice field, which was parched and dry. Soon the clear spring water was running freely down the channel made by the bamboo stem, into the dry rice field, bringing refreshment to the drooping, dry plants.

So the bamboo tree died and brought new life to the master's rice field. The rice grew tall and strong and in turn, for year after year, brought life to many people.

Chapter 8

Everywhere a story

Overview of content

The following short histories of Christians down the ages and up to the present day explore the courage and faith that helped to grow the worldwide Church. Go to www.barnabasinschools.org.uk/whereintheworld/ to find downloadable pictures of these people.

Using the stories with children

Each story offers children the opportunity to hear and/or read about how the Christian faith has motivated people in different parts of the world to make a difference for good because of their faith. If you are using a story in the classroom or as part of collective worship, you might like to use some of the following questions to initiate discussion.

- Which part of this story did you enjoy the most?
- Which part of this story surprised you?
- Which part of this story puzzled you?
- If you could have been in this story, who would you have been and what would you have done?
- If you could draw a picture of one part of this story, what would it be?
- Is there any part of this story that you would like to change?
- What do you think this story tells us about what Christians believe?
- What do you think this story tells us about what God might be like?

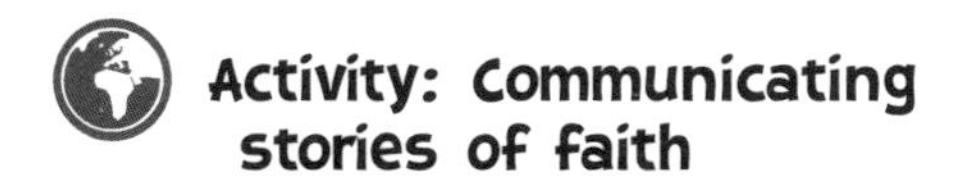

Activity: Communicating stories of faith

Explore further by creatively reshaping the story:

- Turn the story into a short play, based on a series of freeze-frames of key moments in the narrative.
- Rewrite the story as a short newspaper report with a suitable headline and picture.
- Imagine the story is to be made into a blockbuster film and design a poster to advertise it.

Activity: Letters to heroes of faith

The heroes of these stories weren't perfect. They sometimes made bad decisions and certainly made mistakes. Imagine what their friends and family might have said, to try to discourage them from going on with what they felt God had asked of them, and write it in a letter.

Activity: Stories of faith: word-art

In each of these stories, the individual Christians involved were inspired and motivated by their faith. Looking back over the story, try to discover what the people involved believed about God. What were the most important aspects of their Christian faith and how were they expressed in practical ways?

In groups, decide on four or five key words for each story. Beneath the name of the Christian hero of that story, write out the values they stood for. Then turn the words into pieces of decorative word-art that capture, in colour and design, the spirit of the story.

Activity: Stories of faith: logos

Discuss what the children admire most about the Christian faith of the people in the story. If these people were alive and working in their schools and communities today, what difference would they be making? What injustices would they be challenging? How might they apply their Christian faith to what is going on around them?

After reading one or two stories, in groups, list the qualities that make a Christian hero. What symbols or logos can the children think of to express the qualities they list?

*****

Barnabas has published two useful books that supplement and support this chapter:

- *Story Assemblies of 24 Saints* by Heather Butler: www.brfonline.org.uk/9781841017037/
- *Stories of Everyday Saints* by Veronica Heley: www.brfonline.org.uk/9780857460721/

There are also lesson and assembly outlines about famous Christians on www.barnabasinschools.org.uk. Search for the following key words:

- Janani Lawum
- Cross of St George
- Elizabeth Fry
- St Francis
- Salvation Army (or William Booth)
- Johann Sebastian Bach
- William Tyndale

The stories

St Columba

In the sixth century AD, Celtic Christianity began to spread. Columba and a group of his followers travelled north from Ireland to establish a community on the Scottish island of Iona, off the Isle of Mull. From this base, Columba took the story of Jesus out to the Scottish tribes.

Many monks were trained on Iona and later became leaders of abbeys in northern England. From there, they travelled on foot to tell people about Jesus, often baptising whole communities who decided to adopt the new faith. Among these travelling monks were men like Aiden and Cuthbert of Lindisfarne (Holy Island, Northumberland), where the story of Jesus was also written down in beautiful script to make illustrated Gospels that have survived to this day.

Miraculous tales often grew up around the lives of these Celtic saints. Although the stories may be much exaggerated, they show us how highly regarded these first Christian leaders were in Britain.

For example, an early legend about the Loch Ness monster involves Columba. On his way to visit a king in Inverness, he met some people burying the remains of one of their own men, who had been badly savaged by a creature from the loch. The dead man's boat lay on the other side of the water, so Columba ordered one of his followers to swim over and retrieve the boat. As he was swimming, the man was attacked by a creature that reared out of the loch. Columba called on God and commanded the beast to leave. It immediately vanished beneath the waters of the loch, leaving the swimming man unharmed.

St Augustine

After the conversion of the Emperor Constantine to Christianity in the fourth century AD, the Christian church became established in most Mediterranean countries. It was a period of consolidation, but the faith was still on the move. Although there was already a Christian presence in parts of Britain, Pope Gregory in Rome decided to send Christians there to evangelise all its people and to establish the Roman tradition of worship and church organisation.

Augustine led this mission at the end of the sixth century. He was given the wise advice to embrace and baptise local traditions wherever possible, rather than always confronting them as false or demonic. This respect for the local culture was an important aspect of Augustine's success and, sadly, was often forgotten in future Christian missions around the world. Celtic and Roman Christianity met head to head and, at a special council in Whitby, rules for the whole church were adopted that governed faith and practice in Great Britain for centuries to come.

St Cyril and St Methodius

The story of Jesus was taken into northern parts of Europe as well. Cyril and Methodius were brothers from Macedonia, where there were a fair number of Slavs from central Europe. These two Christians learned the Slavic language and so became ideal candidates to take the story further north into the modern Czech Republic and Slovakia, and to the Khazars, north of the Black Sea.

To help establish the Christian faith in these new territories, the brothers decided to translate the Bible into the local language, but that wasn't as simple as it might sound. No written form of Slavic existed, so the two men had to invent a new alphabet. Cyril gives his name to the 'Cyrillic' script, which is still used today, and their Bible and prayer books became a significant influence in taking the Christian story even further into north-eastern Europe and Russia.

Old Church Slavonic was used as the liturgical language of the Russian Orthodox Church between the ninth and twelfth centuries. A more modern form of the language, known as Church Slavonic, appeared during the 14th century and is still used in the Russian Orthodox Church today.

Prince Vladimir

In the year 987, Prince Vladimir of Kiev sent envoys to report on the merits of the faiths of neighbouring nations. By this time, Christianity in the Middle East and North Africa had largely been supplanted by Islam as practised throughout the growing Ottoman Empire. On hearing his envoys, Vladimir settled on Christianity, chiefly because they had witnessed Christian worship at the church in Constantinople, which had so impressed them that they had decided that Christianity must be the true faith. Describing the majestic Divine Liturgy in the church of Hagia Sophia, they are reported as saying, 'We no longer knew whether we were in heaven or on earth. Never was such beauty, and we know not how to tell of it.'

Vladimir was baptised, taking the Christian name of Basil. On his return to his homeland, he established many churches and monasteries. The fact that the Orthodox Christian faith survived the atheism of communist Russia during the 20th century has its roots in that momentous decision of Vladimir, over 1000 years earlier.

This is a good example of the power of individual leaders to influence the faith choice of a whole country, which was a feature of the first millennium of Christianity in Europe.

St Francis

During the Middle Ages, the Christian church in Europe was well established, concerning itself more with maintenance than mission. It was all centred on Rome. Networks of monasteries grew up, which were local expressions of ministry and service to the community—places where people could find regular worship, hospitality, safety and medical help. In the great Benedictine and Augustinian abbeys, monks committed themselves to a religious life of prayer and commitment to God.

Francis is perhaps the best-known of the Christian saints from this period, and possibly the best-loved, because he cared for animals as well as people. Pictures usually show him surrounded by all sorts of creatures. Francis grew up in a very well-to-do Italian home and he fought as a soldier when he was young. However, a period of time as a prisoner and, later, a serious illness made him rethink his attitude to life and he became excited and captivated by the story of Jesus. One day in particular, he felt that God was calling him to 'rebuild God's Church' and, in response, he became a poor travelling preacher, devoting his life to those in need and to prayer. Others joined him in his way of life and soon a whole missionary movement grew up, known today as the Franciscan Order. Many tales are told of his exploits, a number of which include his concern for animals and his delight in God's gift of creation. Francis was always eager to tell others about Jesus and it is Francis we can thank for the invention of the Christmas crib: he was the first to use it to tell the Christmas story.

At the same time as Francis lived, the Islamic faith had spread and become established all along the coast of North Africa, the Middle East and even Turkey. Sadly, the Christian Church in the West saw this only as an attack upon Christendom, and the leaders of Christian Europe chose to set out on a series of bloody Crusades in order to recapture Jerusalem. This did much damage to relationships between Muslims and Christians and has left a legacy of fear and mistrust right up to the present day.

Francis, however, was committed to the way of peace and non-violence, and he lived out his Christian principles with courage, particularly when he set out on a peace mission to meet the leader of the Muslim forces in Jerusalem. This approach to mission was exceptional and stood in contrast to what many Christians at the time felt was the way to approach people of other faiths.

This famous prayer is attributed to St Francis:

Lord, make me an instrument of your peace.
Where there is hatred, let me sow love.
Where there is injury, pardon.
Where there is doubt, faith.
Where there is despair, hope.
Where there is darkness, light.
Where there is sadness, joy.
O Divine Master,
grant that I may not so much seek to be consoled as to console;
to be understood as to understand;
to be loved as to love.
For it is in giving that we receive.
It is in pardoning that we are pardoned,
and it is in dying that we are born to eternal life.
Amen

Bishop Bartolome

The Christian empires of Europe wanted to expand their power and influence. Italy, Spain and Portugal in particular sent out explorers and traders to discover new routes to the riches of Asia that did not involve travelling right around Africa. In so doing, they came to the 'new world' of Latin America. Sadly, the desire to conquer new territory and greed for its mineral wealth became entangled with the attempt to bring the Christian faith to the newly colonised nations, and many atrocities took place in the name of Christianity.

There were, however, Christian voices speaking out against this approach. Bartolome de las Casas took part in the Spanish army expedition to conquer Hispaniola in the Caribbean. He and his fellow soldiers were rewarded with plots of land for farming and mining—and, of course, local Indians were given to them as their slaves. Bartolome spoke up on behalf of the slaves, believing that they should be treated as fellow human beings. He even travelled back to Spain to plead his case with the Spanish government and was given a commission to oversee the fair treatment of the Indians. He met much opposition and, unfortunately, the commission was later disbanded. Nevertheless, Bishop Bartolome, as he had become, continued to act as the conscience of the Spanish new world throughout his long life, and he helped Spain take steps towards treating the Indians fairly.

Other priests also fought for the rights of the indigenous people, facing up to threats and ridicule from the conquistadors. Many recognised the innate spirituality of the Indians and spent time teaching them to read and write and developing their natural abilities as musicians. A large number of Latin American religious songs were written, using local rhythms and musical styles as well as words in the native languages of the peoples of Mexico and Peru.

Francis Xavier

In the 15th and 16th centuries AD, many new religious orders and movements kept appearing in the Christian church in Europe, often pioneered by men and women who longed to take the story of Jesus even further afield and to show Christian compassion to the poor and needy. Francis Xavier was one of the first six members of the Society of Jesus, known as the Jesuits, and was a friend of its founder, Ignatius of Loyola.

Following the routes of Portugal's traders, Francis travelled in Asia for eleven years as a missionary, initially opposed to all non-Western customs. Later, he changed his mind and protested against many of the cruel practices of European government officials that discredited the church and the Christian faith that was being shared with local people.

Francis spent many years among the pearl fishers along the coast near Goa in southern India, learning their language and defending them bravely from the attacks of robbers who came armed with Portuguese weapons. Francis stood up to exploitation with only his faith and the cross of Jesus as his defence and thus won the local people's loyalty and trust. As a result, there is a Christian community there to this day.

Francis travelled further east. He was the very first European to set foot in the empire of Japan and tell the Japanese about Jesus. He eventually died of an illness while attempting to enter the mysterious land of China.

Matteo Ricci

Another Jesuit missionary was Matteo Ricci, who worked in China but had to wait 17 years before he received permission to enter the Imperial City of Peking (now Beijing). He used his skills as a clock repairer and map maker and soon became a Chinese scholar and linguist. He tried to make Christianity as Chinese as possible and to find Chinese equivalents for Christian terms. One of the books he wrote in Chinese led to the first conversions to Christianity in Korea many years later. He honoured Confucius as a holy teacher and regarded Chinese ancestor-worship only as an expression of respect for the great people of the past.

Ricci trusted Chinese Christians themselves to make the final decisions about what they could or could not do. In this respect, he was way ahead of his time, able to separate the heart of what Christians believe from the cultural context within which it is often unhelpfully encased. It was only many centuries later that a missionary to China called Hudson Taylor adopted a similar approach to sharing the story of Jesus cross-culturally.

Here is a story about Matteo Ricci's arrival in China:

Matteo's boat creaked as it sailed. Just ahead, green and rocky, lay the coast of China and the city of Canton. It was 1582 and Matteo Ricci, an Italian missionary in the Roman Catholic Church, had longed to come to Cathay (as China was then called). God, he felt, had called him long ago to preach about Christ to the Chinese and share all he had learnt about science, astronomy and mathematics. Canton's city walls were 40 feet high but, once he was inside, the view took his breath away. He saw wide, straight streets, far better than any in Europe. There were shops everywhere, selling wine, fruit and steaming rice. Important men, dressed in long silk gowns, were carried past in sedan chairs. Every ceiling and wall was an explosion of colours—gold, green, blood red and pearly blue. The governor of the city gave Matteo and his friends a piece of land on which to build a house. 'Meanwhile, pray to heaven for me,' he said.

For years, Matteo worked here, but his dream was to meet Wan Li, the Emperor himself. If only he would believe in Christ, the whole of China would be won! Matteo sent him presents: a small painting of Jesus, a clock and many other things. The picture astonished

Wan Li. It was so real. But for a long time Matteo heard nothing from the Emperor. Then one day, a servant came. 'Come quickly. The clock has stopped.' Soon Matteo was standing where no European had ever stood before—inside the Emperor's palace, in the Forbidden City. Before him towered gateways. Wide courtyards and marble terraces led to brilliant red temples. A lakeside garden was filled with tigers, leopards and bears. Matteo was overjoyed to teach the Emperor's mathematicians how the clock worked. The Emperor, too, was delighted with his gift and sent his servants to ask Matteo questions about his home. What did people wear? What did they eat? What were their houses like? Wan Li watched everything from behind a screen, always hidden.

Matteo worked on in China until his death. Many learned people came to hear of Jesus through him, a humble and gifted man, who never forgot his wonder for China's many riches and yet who also believed that the Christian faith, far from taking away from this, had so much to add.

BASED ON A CMS CHINA RESOURCE PACK FOR CHURCHES

William Brewster and Squanto

From the 14th century onwards, various Christian protest movements began to break away from the Catholic Church governed from Rome. Their leaders questioned many of the Church's doctrines and practices. These 'protestant groups' were also linked to a new nationalism that led some countries to sever their allegiance to the old Holy Roman Empire.

New denominations came into being, such as the Church of England and the Lutheran Church of northern Europe, which experienced further division, particularly as individuals now had the Bible available in their own languages and people could make their own interpretations of scripture. Those who disagreed with the Church of England, for example, were called dissenters and suffered discrimination, which led some of them to leave England for good to begin a new life in the Colonies—now North America.

Of course, they took their Christian story with them.

William Brewster was one of those aboard the *Mayflower* in 1620, who struggled to establish a settlement in the New World. They managed to do so only with the help of the local Native American chief and one of his braves called Squanto, who in time came to hear about Jesus. As the new American nation slowly emerged, the story was taken west, although it was not always shared sensitively with the Native Americans. Once again, the imperative of conquest and fear of the indigenous peoples rode roughshod over those who had a rich spirituality of their own, and much damage was done in the name of Christianity.

Squanto's full name was Tisquantum and he had led an adventurous life, having been taken to Europe as a slave but eventually escaping and working his way back to his homeland. He helped the Pilgrim Fathers recover from the extremely hard first winter by teaching them the native method of maize cultivation. This method used local herring to fertilise the crops. Squanto also taught the colonists how to catch herring, along with eels and other local wildlife.

Samuel Crowther

One of the greatest evils of the 17th and 18th centuries was the slave trade. Thousands of West Africans were taken in slave ships to work on the sugar plantations of the Caribbean, which in turn provided a lucrative trade for the merchants of Europe. Sadly, many Christians were involved in this trade, and it took the brave protests and boycotts of Christians in the Society of Friends (the Quakers) and the political campaigning of men such as William Wilberforce to remind them of the Christian truth that all people are brothers and sisters, created equal in God's sight. Eventually, Parliament in Britain changed the laws about slavery, although discrimination and prejudice continued.

At the beginning of the 19th century, in present-day Nigeria, lived Ajayi with his family. His town was attacked by slave traders and he and his father were taken captive. However, the traders' boat was intercepted by a British patrol and, in accordance with the new Act of Parliament in Britain, the slaves were set free and settled in a colony for free slaves called Sierra Leone, whose capital was Freetown. Ajayi heard about Jesus from local missionaries and was baptised and given a new name: Samuel Crowther.

Samuel worked as a teacher for a while and later joined a trade mission going up the Niger River. He was eager to share his new Christian faith back in his home country and, after training as a Christian minister in England, he returned and established a mission station near his birthplace. He even discovered his mother and sisters still living nearby. Later he was made a bishop—the first black African bishop in the Anglican Church—and began work on a translation of the Bible into his own language of Yoruba.

The Nigerian mission used the local Yoruba language in its worship and witness. This was very significant. It was not the first Bible translation into an African language, but, as Samuel Crowther was the leading influence in its production, it was the first to be made by a native speaker.

William Carey

Increasingly, Protestant missionaries from Europe were travelling to other parts of the world, enthusiastic to share the story of Jesus. They worked initially as chaplains alongside the great trading companies, and this threw up the challenge of how to bring Christianity to local people without also imposing Western cultural values. Many missionaries began to recognise that God had been there before them and that their message was building on an already rich indigenous spirituality, particularly in India.

In 1792, the Baptist missionary William Carey wrote passionately about the need to fulfil the great commission—Jesus' instruction to his friends to go into all the world and make disciples. At the same time he urged Christians to care for indigenous peoples, urging them not to buy sugar from the traders who used slaves. As a result of his time spent in India, William Carey became a professor of the Sanskrit and Bengali languages. He also classified Indian plants in botanic gardens. Another missionary scholar, Henry Martyn, translated the New Testament into Urdu. These two and many others developed real partnerships with the local people and took an interest in their well-being, beyond just religious matters. Hospitals and schools were set up with a particular concern for the poor and marginalised.

Apolo Kivebulaya

At the end of the 19th century, Manubi lived in south-west Uganda and heard the stories of Jesus from a CMS missionary called Alexander Mackay. He was baptised, taking the name Apolo. He was fascinated by what lay beyond the 'Mountains of the Moon' to the west of his country and decided that he wanted to share the Christian faith with the people who lived there. He set off across the Ruwenzori mountains into what is now the Democratic Republic of the Congo and worked among the Pygmy peoples. He particularly loved children and young people and became a popular teacher and minister, wearing his distinctive red jacket, for which he earned the nickname 'Kivebulaya' (which means 'something from another place'). He also wore a tall hat, which saved his life one day when he was fired on with a poison dart.

A church grew up in the town of Bogo, where today there is a cathedral dedicated to Apolo, with an altar made of wood from the trees he planted in the area. Apolo's gentleness and playfulness are still celebrated and remembered on his special day each year (31 May).

Mary Slessor

In the latter half of the 19th century, many women became involved in spreading the Christian faith around the globe. Mary Slessor, from Scotland, went to live among the Efik and Okoyong peoples in Calabar, which is in present-day Nigeria. There she successfully fought against the killing of twins at infancy and cannibalism. She never married but she adopted many African children who had been abandoned by their parents, earning the nickname 'White Ma'.

Mary Slessor was the first woman to appear on the front of a Scottish Clydesdale Bank £10 note. The land and people of Calabar were changed by her heroism. Today her legacy is remembered in both Nigeria and Scotland. She is fondly remembered as 'the White Queen of Calabar'. She died there in 1915 and was given a state burial.

Mary Slessor became an inspiration to all who heard her story. She was not only a pioneer missionary but also a pioneer for women in missions. Today, the Mary Slessor Foundation (MSF) seeks to continue the social and medical work of the great missionary. It aims to improve and attain sustainable developments in the social, economic and health sectors of the community of Akpap Okoyong in the northern part of Cross River State, Nigeria, by funding a skills training centre, a medical facility and an agricultural processing mill.

Benedita da Silva

Born in 1942, Benedita da Silva is an African-Brazilian activist and politician who organised her people in the midst of poverty and despair in Rio de Janeiro.

Born in the shanty towns of the city, da Silva lived with 13 brothers and sisters in extremely poor conditions. As a child, she worked as a live-in maid to support her family and was subjected to abuse. Lacking adequate medical care, she was forced to watch two of her own children die from diseases that could have been treated.

Inspired by these experiences and her strong Christian faith, da Silva knew that her life and the conditions for the poor around her must change. With the help of her neighbours, she set about organising a clean water and sewage system in the slums and even set up a generator to provide electricity. She formed a women's branch of the Rio de Janeiro Federation of Slums. Although she was in her 40s, da Silva went back to school and earned her high school diploma, then her college degree alongside her daughter.

Da Silva went on to become the city's first black councillor. Four years later, she was elected a federal deputy, later a senator, then the first black female governor of Rio. She believed that God created all people to be equal and so blacks and women should be fully involved in Brazilian political life. Benedita da Silva continued to dedicate her life in particular to women and the disadvantaged people of Rio de Janiero.

Desmond Tutu

Desmond Tutu was born in Klerksdorp, South Africa, in 1931. His early life was heavily influenced by the care shown to him and his family by a Catholic missionary, Father Trevor Huddleston. Such care was particularly remarkable because Desmond was black and Trevor was white. In those days, the two races were kept apart under the segregated system known as apartheid. All races and colours lived and worked separately, which led to injustices in housing, education and the law.

As a student, Desmond became a deeply committed Christian. Increasingly the unfairness of the situation in his homeland influenced his career and his activities. He became a church minister in 1967, then Dean of Johannesburg and, later, Bishop of Lesotho. He spoke out against the political system that denied the black majority equal rights in their own land. However, he always preached non-violent opposition, despite having every reason to feel bitter and unforgiving toward the white rulers. His smile and his buoyant character could often defuse an ugly situation. In 1984 he was awarded the Nobel Peace Prize. Two years later he became Archbishop of Cape Town.

Desmond's patient prayer and work for justice came to a head when, in 1994, South Africa elected a new government and apartheid was officially ended. Desmond Tutu always connected his religious faith with the realities around him. The Bible teaches us that God made all people equal and that forgiveness and love are stronger than bitterness and hatred. He played a leading role in bringing apartheid to an end and, since then, has continued to help many people come to terms with the scars and unforgiveness that still mark their lives because of all that has happened in the past. Christians believe that God can give people strength to forgive and the power to live differently and justly in the world.

Desmond believes that faith should affect all we do and help make this world a better place. He once said, 'Our Christianity is not something we put on like our Sunday best, only for Sundays; it is for every day. We are Christians Monday to Monday.'

Chapter 9

Everywhere a friend

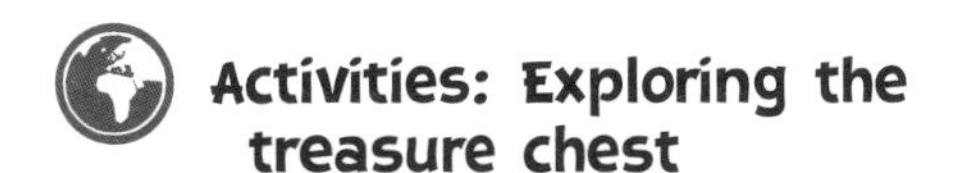

Overview of content

In our unequal world, it is always a challenge to build partnerships with churches and schools overseas that are genuinely reciprocal. This chapter includes an African fable that explores this challenge; it also offers guidelines for teachers about learning about, from and with the worldwide Christian family. Finally there is a template for an experiential workshop about reciprocal partnership with churches and schools outside the UK.

A story to use with children

Pentecost was the moment when, through the Holy Spirit, Christians found a new unity and power to work together for the growth of the kingdom of God. Each believer discovered that he or she had gifts from God that complemented other people's gifts so that the work could be done. What is true for individuals is also true for the different branches of the Christian church around the world. The apostle Paul uses the image of the human body to express this truth. In 1 Corinthians 12:7 he writes, 'The Spirit has given each of us a special way of serving others.'

The following story tries to explore this image through an animal fable from Africa. If you use the story in the classroom or as part of collective worship, you will find the following guidance helpful.

- Print off from the internet some simple visuals for the four animals (enlarged computer clip art, for example). You will need pictures of a warthog, a giraffe, a lion and a toucan.
- Try to work out a different voice to use for each of these animals as you tell the story. Also, involve the children in some appropriate sound effects at the right moments.
- Don't rush to tell the children the 'moral' of the tale, but let them think about it for themselves. Just what was the 'treasure chest'?

Activities: Exploring the treasure chest

Classes could be invited to work with this story in a number of ways:

- Act out the story in groups.
- Retell the story from just one animal's point of view.
- On an outline drawing of an open treasure chest, draw or write about some of the treasures that the children think the animals found by working together.
- Underneath an illustration of one moment from the story, write about what the story means for them personally.
- Write a parable or fable of their own, using people or objects from their own community that illustrate the discovery of the same treasure.
- Apply the fable to a link with another part of the world that your school has. What strengths and gifts does each bring to the relationship? What can each learn from the other?
- Explore what keeps people from discovering the treasure of true partnership. How might the end of the story be rewritten to illustrate this?

Story: The treasure chest

Once upon a time, deep in a jungle far away, there was a large open area of grassland. This wide clearing was surrounded in each direction by the tall, dense trees of the rainforest. Right in the centre of the open land was a tall baobab tree with its great chunky branches stretching outwards and upwards, like an ancient king proudly showing to the other trees his special kingdom from his throne at the centre.

In fact, each of the four edges to this open land was a boundary to other kingdoms, each the territory of four of the more colourful animals of the forest world. One side was ruled by the Giraffe, one by the Lion, one by the Toucan and the other by the Warthog.

In her kingdom the Giraffe walked slowly, with her neck stretched up high, chewing at the leaves she could take from the topmost branches of her part of the forest.

In his kingdom the Lion walked cautiously with a stately manner, growling from time to time as he surveyed his part of the forest.

In his kingdom the Toucan flapped his wings constantly as he hopped from branch to branch, eyeing all that went on in his part of the forest.

In her kingdom the Warthog shambled along awkwardly, snorting and sniffing as she made her way clumsily through her part of the forest.

Now, the amazing thing was that whenever any of the four animals reached the edge of his or her forest world, they would all come to an abrupt halt. They never went any further than their forest boundary. None of them ever went on to the open grassland that belonged to the baobab tree.

And that was how things always were. Each minded his or her own business. They didn't acknowledge each other. They didn't talk to each other. In fact, they quite positively kept away from each other, viewing the other three animals with suspicion. After all, what need was there to step beyond their part of the forest? Didn't they each have the very best bit? Wasn't their forest by far the most comfortable, interesting and suitable to their particular needs? There was no need to cross the clearing and visit the other parts, and so they never did. The Giraffe enjoyed reaching up to the leaves high in her trees; the Lion enjoyed snoozing in the long grasses beneath his trees; the Toucan enjoyed the rich greenery and excellent perches high up in his trees; the Warthog enjoyed squelching through the muddy ground at the foot of her trees. And so life went on, until...

One night there was an almighty crash that woke up the whole rainforest for miles around. It came from the clearing, and it had something to do with the great baobab tree.

By the pale light of dawn, each of the animals crept to the edge of their part of the forest to see what it could be. There was no mistaking the source of that midnight sound. There, high up in the branches of the great tree was an object, gleaming as it caught the first rays of the sun. It was a beautiful decorated chest... a treasure chest. It had a carved lid and a golden lock, and there were thick ropes around it for added security. 'It must contain a very rich treasure,' thought each of the animals to themselves. 'It must be a gift from heaven and... it could be mine.' It would mean entering the clearing, but it was too great a prize to lose because of fear.

Cautiously each animal, who had been thinking exactly the same about the treasure, stepped forward together towards the tree, each from his or her side of the forest.

The Giraffe looked up at the chest, high in the baobab's branches. 'Well, the height is no problem for me. I could easily reach the chest, but what about those thick ropes, the heavy carved lid and that golden lock?' thought the Giraffe. 'I'd better wait and see what the others will do.'

The Lion looked up at the chest, high in the baobab's branches. 'Well, those thick ropes will be no problem. I could easily shake them loose, but what about that golden lock and the heavy carved lid? And how can I get it down to the ground?' thought the Lion. 'I'd better wait and see what the others will do.'

The Toucan looked up at the chest, high in the baobab's branches. 'Well, that golden lock won't be a problem. I could easily pick it open. But how will I get it down? And what about those thick ropes and that heavy carved lid?' thought the Toucan. 'I'd better wait and see what the others will do.'

The Warthog looked up at the chest, high in the baobab's branches. 'Well, that heavy carved lid won't be a problem. I could easily prize that open with my tusks. But how will I get it down? And what about those thick ropes and the golden lock?' thought the Warthog. 'I'd better wait and see what the others will do.'

And so they waited... and they waited... and they waited. But nobody moved. Then the idea must have come to each of them at the same time. They realised what they would have to do if they wanted to discover the treasure. They exchanged glances, knowing looks and even a smile or two, and then each animal moved up to the tree, closer to the treasure and closer to each other than they had ever been before.

The Giraffe made the first move. Reaching up with her long neck, she prodded the chest with the little horns on her head and, slowly but surely, dislodged it from the branches so that it came crashing down to the ground.

The Lion moved in next and grabbed the thick ropes around the chest in his sharp, fierce teeth. He shook and shook until, slowly but surely, the ropes loosened and he could pull them away from the treasure chest.

The Toucan moved in next. With his long, sharp beak he began to pick at the golden lock, twisting and turning until, slowly but surely, the lock clicked open and the clasp sprang up.

Finally, it was the turn of the Warthog. She moved in and carefully inserted her great big tusks under the lid. Using all her strength, she began, slowly but surely, to prize open the heavy wooden lid to reveal the treasure.

But just as the lid fell back, there was a great crash. It was just like the one they had heard in the night, but this time there came also a blinding flash of light.

When the animals recovered from the glare, they looked for the treasure, but to their amazement it was gone. The chest had disappeared. There was no carved wooden lid, no golden lock, no thick ropes. The treasure chest had completely disappeared.

The four animals looked around in surprise and then looked at each other. It was then that they must all have thought the same thing at the same time, because, slowly but surely, they all began to smile.

They realised that they had discovered the treasure after all. They had discovered it together and, what was more, they still had that treasure—the greatest treasure they could ever have found.

Now, what do you think that treasure is?

Creating and maintaining partnerships with the worldwide Church

Start with your own classroom

Britain is now a multi-national and multi-ethnic country and, in most classrooms, you will find children with links and roots around the world. The fact that your school is already a place to experience the global dimension of faith may well offer the opportunity to nurture very direct and personal links with communities in other countries, some of whom will be Christian. It is important to include these children and their experiences as part of this unit of work.

A useful resource book is *A Life Like Mine: How children live around the world* (Dorling Kindersley, 2006). Its companion volumes, *Children Just Like Me: Celebrations* (DK, 1997) and *Children Just Like Me: A unique celebration of children around the world* (DK, 1995), are also recommended for this theme.

Work in a cross-curricular way

The theme of the worldwide expression of the Christian faith connects very readily with other parts of the primary school curriculum. There are obvious links with history, geography and citizenship: the stories of individual Christians in Chapter 8 and the background to the churches in the swallow's journey (Chapter 2) touch on many such global issues. In addition, there are opportunities to explore:

- **Artwork**: artwork linked to the Christian story is available from all around the world in many styles and traditions (see the suggestions in Chapter 4 and in Appendix 4).
- **Music**: experiencing Christian songs from non-Western cultures offers the opportunity to explore differing musical traditions and indigenous instruments. A useful source of such instruments is www.monkey-drum.co.uk. For worldwide music, see Appendix 1 and www.barnabasinschools.org.uk/whereintheworld/ for support material. You can also use the song 'God is so good' in different languages (see Chapter 2).
- **Story**: all the usual techniques for exploring stories creatively can be applied to the Bible stories and life stories contained in this book, including drama techniques such as hot-seating, conscience circus and freeze-frames. Storytelling has always been a very important way to create community, share information and explore the big questions about life in most of the non-Western world. A number of world stories are included in this book. Another useful resource is *The Lion Book of Wisdom Stories from Around the World* by David Self (Lion Hudson, 2008).
- **Modern languages**: this is one very direct way to make global connections. In the worldwide Christian church, language can both divide and unite: key faith words are shared and easily recognised (for example, peace, praise, God, Jesus and Hallelujah) even though they may sound and look very different. Learning some faith words in new languages can help build bridges. For example, there are some suggestions for games involving greetings and the word for 'peace' in Chapter 5, there are some important festival words in a variety of languages in Chapter 7, and there are songs using other languages with key faith words in Appendix 1.

There is no shortage of freely available information that will support a global perspective on the Christian faith. Magazines from aid and mission agencies, web-based articles (including pictures and YouTube clips) and even brochures from travel agencies can provide helpful material. For a full list of resources, see Appendix 4.

Set up a school-to-school partnership

This is arguably the most rewarding way to facilitate an exploration of the Christian faith from a global perspective and it will directly contribute to helping your children encounter and value difference on an international scale. However, there are some pitfalls of which teachers and schools should be aware. The most helpful place to go for advice and guidance is the British Council Schools Online website (http://schoolsonline.britishcouncil.org), which lists schools on every continent that are keen to form partnerships with British schools. Modern technology means that such links are very easy to set up, but, in some parts of the world, huge inequalities in resources, the ability to communicate regularly and standards of living mean that the links are not always easy to maintain. There is advice at Global Gateway about all this, including guidance about child protection, data security and how to deal with inappropriate subject matter, language or requests for gifts.

It is vital to work hard to make sure that any such links start off and remain reciprocal. This is particularly true where any charity giving as part of the link is concerned. Each school should be both a giver and a receiver.

All sorts of other openings can lead to school-to-school links and are worth exploring:

- Personal links through staff or parents at the schools.
- Local church links with Christians working overseas.
- Diocesan links with partner dioceses in other countries.
- Local town twinning links.
- Charity links of regular fundraising for an overseas cause.

Another risk is that, in making the links, the RE element can be left out. Schools in many parts of the world do not have RE on their curriculum, although that does not mean that faith isn't an important part of the lives of the communities linked to those schools. In fact, in many cases, Christian faith is very much part of the lives of children with whom you will be communicating, so, when letters or e-mails are sent and photos and artefacts exchanged, make sure that this element is included. Children from your partner school will usually be more than willing to tell you about worship in their churches, special festivals and local Christian customs.

Finally, it is worth noting that such partnerships can lead to schools being given the International Schools award, which in turn can attract funding to support and maintain the link. For more information, go to: http://schoolsonline.britishcouncil.org.

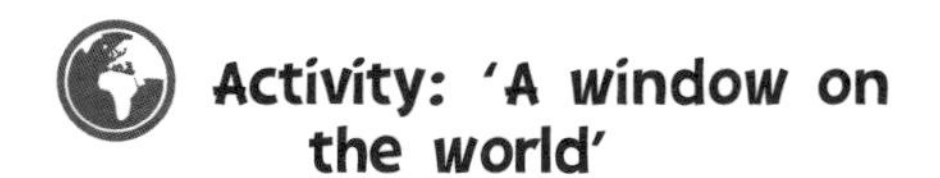

Activity: 'A window on the world'

The following is an outline for a classroom activity to 'visit' another part of the worldwide Church.

Aim

To help the children make creative connections between themselves and children in another part of the developing world, within the framework of a partnership with the Christian Church worldwide.

Objectives

- To explore the similarities and differences between schools and churches in the UK and a different part of the world.
- To experience a day in the life of a primary school child and Christian worship in the developing world.
- To enter imaginatively into the lives of children different from themselves; to do so out of solidarity and respect, not pity and guilt, recognising that in our partnerships with an unequal world there are things we can give each other.
- To empathise with the hopes and fears, joys and sadnesses of children from another part of our world.
- To investigate what the Christian faith has to say about injustice, inequality, loving our neighbours and caring for each other.

Outline for the workshop

Icebreaker

Gather the children in a circle. Play a 'cross the circle' game with children moving across the circle sensibly in response to various statements about where they live; how they travelled to school; where they have travelled in the UK, in Europe and in the rest of the world; what their daily routine normally involves (getting up, breakfast, TV, interests, clothes, sports and so on).

Link to the worldwide theme by saying, 'There are so many things that we have in common and take for granted. In this workshop we are going to travel off in our imaginations and visit another part of the world. I wonder what will be the same and what will be different. I wonder what will be worse and what will be better. I wonder what we will learn from it.'

Travelling away

'Let's travel to... (fill in the name of the country where your link is)!'

Lead an on-the-spot workout—packing luggage, walking to the car, driving to the airport, boarding the plane, taking off, banking left and right, experiencing turbulence, landing, carrying luggage in a different climate, waiting in queues, bumping along in a crowded taxi, setting off to a distant town or village, spotting new sights and sounds, including wildlife and so on.

Sharing everyday life

Divide into groups with five or six children in each. You are now brothers and sisters in different families. In separate 'homes' (each marked by a square on the ground in the workshop area), lie down to sleep. Many homes in the developing world are crowded. Can the children imagine it?

Water challenge

In many parts of the world, children wake early to the sound of a cock crowing at 6 o'clock. For many of them, the first job of the day is a two-mile walk to fetch water. Use large camping bottles filled with water. Organise a challenge, with each member of the three 'families' in turn going to fetch and carry the water.

After that, it is a three-mile walk to school. Children walk around the workshop space several times while you arrange for three wooden benches to be placed in the centre.

At school

Learn some words in the language of your link school by rote.

Often, teaching resources can be hard to come by, so share one book between five. Write names on a piece of paper, but provide only one pencil per group.

Explain that not every child can go to school in some parts of the world. In many places, there is a cost involved, so there are many children who can't afford to go because their families can't pay for a uniform or for very basic equipment. Some children have to stay at home to work in the fields for the family. Those who do go to school count it a great privilege. Ask the group what they think of that.

Play

Children in many countries can't afford basic toys or sports equipment. In groups, make a football by scrunching sheets of newspaper into a ball (just as banana leaves are used in parts of Africa, for example). Use string or tape to hold the ball together. Play catch with the ball.

Story time

Tell a participative story from another part of the world, such as this one from Tanzania. Illustrate the story by providing a bunch of green garden canes and inviting the children to do as the mother in the story says.

Once in Tanzania, during a long period of drought, there was a mother who had become very ill, so times had become doubly hard for her family. One morning she sent out her three children to gather sticks for the kitchen fire. They much preferred to have the time to themselves but their mother explained that without the fire they couldn't cook, and without some food they would all grow too weak to carry on.

The children set off, each one slowly gathering a bundle that they eventually brought back home. They were tired from their efforts and their mother sensed that they slightly resented having to work together like this, so she called them to her, each one with the bundle of sticks they had collected.

First she asked her youngest child to try to break the bundle of sticks in two for the fire. The girl tried her hardest but had no success.

'Pass the bundle to your brother,' said their mother. 'Let him have a go.'

The brother also tried his hardest but could not break the sticks.

'Let me try,' said their big sister.

So the bundle was passed on again, but even the eldest and strongest child could not break the sticks for the fire.

Then their mother asked them to pass the sticks to her. She untied the bundle and handed out just one stick at a time to her children. 'Now try breaking the sticks,' she said with a smile.

Stick by stick, the children had no difficulty in breaking the bundles of sticks for the fire.

'Now do you see why it is so important that we work together?' asked their mother. 'Never forget this saying: Umoja ni nguvu (Unity is strength).'

Christian worship

Sing a simple Christian song from another country (see the suggestions in Appendix 1). Explore a Bible story that has links to the growth of the worldwide Church, such as Jesus' parable of the mustard seed (Matthew 13:31–32). There is a Godly Play™ reflective version of this parable in *The Complete Guide to Godly Play Volume 3* by Jerome W. Berryman (Living the Good News, 2002).

Home... work

The long walk home (repeat the circling of the workshop space) is often followed not by homework and TV but hard work on the family allotment. Mime some hard digging and then try another fun challenge—carry some items, such as vegetables or fruits, on their heads. (You will need a small shallow basket or a piece of cloth to use as a platform.)

Gathering round 'the fire'

Bring your imaginary day in another country to an end by having a time of reflection around the 'outdoor fire'.

- I wonder what part of this day you liked the best.
- I wonder which part of life for a child your age in [country] is better than life here in the UK. Which part is worse?

- What do you think a child in [country] might say about our life in the UK?
- I wonder what one thing you would like to give children in [country] if you had the money and skills. What would you like them to give you?

Travelling back home

Reverse the actions described at the beginning of this outline.

– Appendix 1 –

Everywhere a song and a prayer

The following songs from the world church have been chosen because they are easy to learn. Even where there are other languages involved, the words aren't too complicated.

The world prayers in this section are all short and are therefore useful for the classroom, for display or for use in collective worship. Usually there is a flavour of the local culture in the imagery used.

World worship: Songs

In Chapter 2 of this book, there are a number of versions of the chorus 'God is so good' in various languages (*Junior Praise* No 53). Here are a few more versions.

- **Urdu (Pakistan)**: Khudawand bhala hai (x 3), bhala hai Yesu
- **Russian**: Bog tak veleek (x 3), ohn menyah lyubeet
- **Kinyarwanda (Rwanda)**: Imana ni nzi-za (x 3), ni nzi-za cya-ne
- **Japanese**: Shu wa su-ba-ra-shii (x 3),Wa-ta-shi no Shu
- **Tamil**: Jesu Nallavar (x 3), Nallavar Yenakku
- **Nigeria (Yoruba)**: Oluwa dara (x 3), dara fun mi
- **Pidgin (Papua New Guinea)**: God I gut pela (x 3), God I gut long mi
- **Nepal**: Ishwar asal chan (x 3), malai dyya gharchan

Here is a Chinese version of 'God is so good' with three additional verses.

Shen jiu shi ai (x 3) (God is love)
Ta zhe yang ai wo (This is how he loves me)

Chui ting wo qiu (x 3) (He answers prayer)
Ta zhe yang ai wo (This is how he loves me)

Ta shi wo zhu (x 3) (He is my Lord)
Ta zhe yang ai wo (This is how he loves me)

Ta kuai zai lai (x 3) (He's coming again soon)
Ta zhe yang ai wo (This is how he loves me)

From Africa

- Amen Siakudumisa (South Africa)
- Jesus tawa pano (Zimbabwe)
- He came down (Cameroons)
- Wa Wa Wa Emimimo (Nigeria)
- Thuma Mina (South Africa)
- Imela (Nigeria)
- If you believe and I believe (Zimbabwe)

From Latin America

- Santo (Argentina)
- Sent by the Lord (Nicaragua)
- Gloria (Peru)

From the Caribbean

- Halle, Halle, Halle

From India

- Yesuve Saranam
- Jesus the Lord said

From Korea

- Come now, O prince of Peace

These songs can be found in the books *Many and Great*, *Sent by the Lord* and *In Every Corner Sing* (see Resources on page 82).

There are some indigenous versions of the chorus 'This is the day'. The following is from Pakistan, in Urdu.

Yehee hai din (x 2) (This is the day)
Jo Khud-avard ka hai (x 2)
(That the Lord has made)
Hum hongay shaad (x 2) (We will rejoice)
Aur Khushi Karen-ge (x 2) (And be glad in it)
Yehee hai din jo Khud-avard ka hai
(This is the day that the Lord has made)
Hum hongay shaad aur khushi karen-g
(We will rejoice and be glad in it)
Yehee hai din (x 2) (This is the day)
Jo Khud-avard ka hai (That the Lord has made)

This is a version of the same song from Nepal:

Aja ko din (x 2)
Unle sree je ka (x 2)
Romaundai jaun (x 2)
Khushee manow (x 2)
Aja ko din unle sree je ka
Romaunda jaun khushee manow
Aja ko din (x 2)
Unle sree je ka

Here is an Arabic version of 'Sing Hallelujah to the Lord' (*Mission Praise* 601), from the Middle East:

Shokran lelrub, Hallelujah (x 4)
(Thanks to the Lord)
Hamdan lelrub, Hallelujah (x 4)
(Praise to the Lord)
Magdan lelrub, Hallelujah (x4)
(Glory to the Lord)
Haigi tani elrub, Hallelujah (x4)
(The Lord is coming soon)

World worship: world prayers

O God, grant that always,
at all times and in all places,
in all things both small and great,
we may ever do your most holy will
and be Jesus Christ's faithful servants
and handmaids to our lives' end. Amen

A PRAYER FROM BANGLADESH

Saturate me with the oil of the Spirit, that I may be a flame. But flame is transient, often short-lived. Can you bear this, my soul—a short life? In me there dwells the Spirit of the Great Short-Lived, whose zeal for God's house consumed him. Make me your fuel, Flame of God.

A PRAYER FROM URUGUAY

Bless, O Lord, the plants, the vegetation, and the herbs of the field, that they may grow and increase to fullness and bear much fruit. And may the fruit of the land remind us of the spiritual fruit we should bear. Amen

We pray, Lord, for the rising of the water of the Nile this year. May Christ, our Saviour, bless it and raise it, cheering the earth and sustaining us, his creatures. And may the rising water remind us of the living water, freely given to all who repent and believe.

TWO PRAYERS FROM THE COPTIC ORTHODOX LITURGY, EGYPT

I read
in a book
that a man called
Christ
went about doing good.
It is very disconcerting
to me
that I am so easily
satisfied
with just
going about.

A PRAYER FROM JAPAN

God, you are the God of life.
Transform us in the depths of our hearts
into people through whom your peace
is carried out into your world.

Send your Spirit into the hearts of those
who are captured in the net of violence,
be it as perpetrators or as victims,
and let us never give up the search
for the chance to talk to them.

A PRAYER FROM CROATIA

O Christ, as we follow you
down the road to Calvary,
guide us to become active participants,
not curious bystanders.
O Christ, as we stand
with the mourners at the cross,
give us the love that can forgive those
who trespass against us.
O Christ, as we witness the new life given to us
through your resurrection,
empower us with faith to act
and spread the good news.

A PRAYER FROM JERUSALEM

Come, Holy Spirit
Come, Holy Spirit,
teacher of the humble, judge of the arrogant.
Come, hope of the poor, refreshment of the weary,
rescuer of the shipwrecked.
Come, most splendid adornment
of all living beings,
the sole salvation of all who are mortal.
Come, Holy Spirit, have mercy on us,
imbue our lowliness with your power,
meet our weakness with the fullness of your grace.
Come, Holy Spirit, renew the whole creation!

A PRAYER FROM THE ORTHODOX CHURCH

Stay with us, Lord,
for the day is far spent
and we have not yet recognised your face
in each of our brothers and sisters.

Stay with us, Lord
for the day is far spent
and we have not yet shared your bread
in grace with our brothers and sisters.

Stay with us, Lord,
for the day is far spent
and we have not yet listened to your word
on the lips of our brothers and sisters.

Stay with us, Lord,
because our very night becomes day
when you are there.

A PRAYER FROM KOREA

God, it may be worldly wisdom that we should grow less dependent on our mother's anchal as we mature in age. But teach us that it is spiritual wisdom and, indeed, your will for us, that we grow closer to your anchal and hold on to it more fervently, day by day.*

May we have your wisdom, courage and, at times, temerity to wave your anchal so high above everything else that all can discern its graceful patterns and admire its gorgeous designs. And God, make sure that your anchal for ever flows longer and wider, that it embraces all children around the world in its loving and intricate folds.

A PRAYER FROM PAKISTAN
(* The anchal is the edge of the sari)

Lord, please go before us, to lead:
walk beside us, to befriend;
be above us, to protect;
stay behind us, to direct;
be beneath us, to support;
abide with us to love.

FROM SOUTH AFRICA: A PRAYER WRITTEN IN PRISON

Thank you, God. You called me and asked me to spread your love and gospel, just as Jesus Christ called his disciples and asked them to spread the gospel.

We pray that we may spread the gospel to our neighbourhood and brothers and sisters, in spiritual truth and with a true heart.

We hope that Jesus Christ's love will be with us and that the fruit of mission will be borne wherever we go.

In the name of Jesus Christ we pray, who leads us, his servants. Amen

A PRAYER FROM KOREA

In thy journeys to and fro
God direct thee;
In thy happiness and pleasure
God bless thee;
In care, anxiety, or trouble
God sustain thee;
In peril and in danger
God protect thee.

A PRAYER FROM NIGERIA

Let us give thanks to the Lord
in the day of devastation;
Let us give thanks to the Lord
in the day of contentment.
Jesus has bound the world round
with the pure light of the Word of the Father.
When we beseech the Lord and unite our hearts
and have hope, then the evil spirit has no power.
God has not forgotten us.
Evil is departing and holiness is advancing.
These are the things that shake the earth.

A PRAYER FROM SUDAN

God of all people, we yearn for peace in our land,
That we may pray to you in freedom:
This is the prayer we make:
Hear our prayers as we cry out to you,
Hear the wailing of our souls in the wilderness.
Watch over us, our Creator.

A DINKA PRAYER

O God,
Be the canoe that holds me up in the sea of life;
Be the rudder that keeps me on a straight course;
Be the outrigger that supports me
in times of great temptation.
Let your Spirit be my sail that carries me
through each day.
Keep my body strong, so I can paddle steadfastly
on in the voyage of life. Amen

A PRAYER FROM MELANESIA

You are the God of the poor,
the human and simple God;
The God who sweats in the street,
the God with a weather-beaten face.
That's why I talk to you
in the way that my people talk,
Because you are the labourer,
the worker Christ. Amen

A PRAYER FROM NICARAGUA

Give us strength to build ever more bridges of
peace all over the world.

A PRAYER FROM TONGA

God the Sender, send us.
God the Sent, come with us.
God the Strengthener of those who go,
empower us,
that we may go for ever and wherever with you,
Father, Son and Holy Spirit.

A PRAYER FROM THE UNITED KINGDOM

O God, grant that your spirit may move us to
enter your temple. Open our eyes that we may see
your saving grace, and stretch forth our hands to
receive the Lord who has come.

A PRAYER FROM CHINA

You can find more world church prayers linked to each of the various countries visited in Chapter 2.

– Appendix 2 –

Everywhere an anniversary

The following anniversaries and special days give us a link with the festivals and celebrations in other countries and could be used as a launch point for your group both to learn from and pray with the worldwide Christian Church.

1 January	Independence Day in Sudan (1956)
2 January	Heroes of Independence Day in Haiti; Samuel Azariah, evangelist
3 January	National Holiday in Upper Volta
4 January	Independence Day in Burma
6 January	The Orthodox Christmas; Children's Day in Uruguay
12 January	Zanzibar Revolution Day in Tanzania (1946)
13 January	Liberation Day in Togo; Redemption Day in Ghana
17 January	St Anthony of Egypt
20 January	National Heroes' Day in Brazil; Army Day in Mali
26 January	Republic Day in India; National Day in Australia
Last Sunday in January	World Leprosy Day
Last weekend in January	World Peace Weekend
Third week in January	Week of Prayer for Christian Unity
Third Monday in January	Martin Luther King Day

Chinese New Year falls in January or February.

1 February	Holiday in Malaysia
3 February	Heroes' Day in Mozambique; Saints and Martyrs in Europe
4 February	National Day in Sri Lanka
6 February	New Zealand Day (Treaty of Waitangi in 1840 between British and Maoris)
7 February	Independence Day in Grenada
11 February	Nelson Mandela released in 1990; Youth Day in Cameroon; National Foundation Day in Japan
12 February	Union Day in Burma
14 February	Cyril and Methodius, missionaries in Eastern Europe
15 February	Orthodox Youth Day
17 February	Founding of the Red Cross (1863); Janani Luwum, Archbishop of Uganda
18 February	Republic Day in the Gambia; Democracy Day in Nepal
21 February	Saints and Martyrs of Africa
26 February	National Day in Kuwait
27 February	Independence Day, Dominican Republic (1844); Statehood Day, St Kitts (1967)
1st Sunday in February	Homelessness Sunday
3rd Sunday in February	Unemployment Sunday

1 March	St David's Day; Heroes' Day in Paraguay
2 March	St Chad
3 March	Martyrs Day in Malawi; National Day in Morocco
5 March	National Day in Equatorial Guinea
6 March	Independence Day in Ghana (1951)
8 March	Women's Day in Guinea Bissau; International Women's Day; National Day in Libya
12 March	Independence Day in Mauritius (1968)
15 March	Youth Day in Zambia
17 March	St Patrick's Day; World Maritime Day
20 March	Independence Day, Tunisia; St Cuthbert
21 March	National Tree Planting Day, Lesotho
22 March	World Day for Water; Emancipation Day in Puerto Rico (abolition of slavery in 1873)
23 March	Pakistan Day (1956)
25 March	Independence Day in Greece; Feast of the Good Thief
26 March	Independence Day, Bangladesh
31 March	St Innocent of Alaska (Orthodox missionary)
1st and 2nd week in March	Fair Trade fortnight
2nd Monday in March	Commonwealth Day

1st Friday in March	Women's World Day of Prayer
1 April	Youth Day in Benin
4 April	National Day in Senegal
5 April	Arbor Day in Korea
7 April	World Health Day; Women's Day in Mozambique
8 April	Saints and Martyrs of the Americas
9 April	Martyrs' Day in Tunisia
12 April	CMS Founded in 1799
13 April	Tamil New Year; National Day in Chad
17 April	Independence Day in Syria
19 April	Republican Anniversary Day, Sierra Leone (1971); Independence Day in Venezuela and Zimbabwe
20 April	Captain Cook 'discovers' Australia (1770)
22/23 April	National Sovereignty Days in Turkey
25 April	Portugal Day; National Flag Day, Swaziland
26 April	Union Day, Tanzania (1964)
27 April	Independence Day, Togo (1960) and Sierra Leone
3 May	Constitution Memorial Day, Japan
5 May	Children's Day in Japan and Korea
11 May	CMS Missionary John Rebmann sees Mt Kilimanjaro (1807)
14 May	National Flag Day in Paraguay
15 May	International Day of Families; Independence Day in Paraguay (1811)
17 May	Independence Day in Norway (1814)
18 May	Flag Day, Haiti
19 May	Youth Day, Turkey
20 May	National Holiday, Cameroon
22 May	National Heroes' Day, Sri Lanka
25 May	National Holiday, Argentina; Independence Day, Chad; Africa Day in Mali; Africa Freedom Day in Zambia; Jordan, Independence Day
26 May	National Holiday, Turkey
30 May	Apolo Kivebulaya, evangelist
31 May	World No Tobacco Day; Republic Day, South Africa
3rd week in May	Christian Aid Week
1 June	Children's Day, Mongolia
3 June	Uganda Martyrs' Day
4 June	Day of prayer for Children at Risk; Children's Day, Vietnam
5 June	World Environment Day; Liberation Day, Seychelles
8 June	Opening of the 8-day CMS Africa and the East Exhibition at Islington (¼ million visitors) (1909)
9 June	St Columba
12 June	Independence Day, Philippines (1898)
14 June	Fathers of the Eastern Church
19 June	National Holiday, Algeria
22 June	National Thanksgiving Day, Haiti
25 June	Independence Day in Mozambique
26 June	United Nations Organisation founded 1945; Independence Day in Somalia; International Day against Drug Abuse
27 June	World Diabetes Day
29 June	Samuel Crowther; Independence Day, Seychelles
1 July	Canada Day: John Venn and Henry Venn; Independence Day, Burundi & Rwanda; Republic Day, Ghana (1965)
3 July	Family Day, Lesotho; Independence Day, Algeria (1962)
4 July	Independence Day, USA
5 July	Independence Day, Venezuela (1811); Independence Day, Algeria
6 July	Republic Day in Malawi (1966)
7 July	Farmers' Day in Tanzania; National Day, Equatorial Guinea
10 July	Independence Day, Argentina (1816)
11 July	World Population Day; National Day in Mongolia
14 July	National Day in Iraq; National Holiday, Nicaragua
18 July	Constitution Day, Uruguay (1830); National Holiday, Spain
20 July	National Holiday, Colombia
23 July	National Day in Egypt
26 July	Independence Day, Liberia (1847)
28 July	Independence Day, Peru (1821)
29 July	William Wilberforce (1833)
1st Sunday	Sea Sunday (Mission to Seafarers)
4 August	Foundation of British Red Cross (1870)
6 August	Hiroshima Day; National Holiday, Bolivia
7 August	National Holiday, Colombia
9 August	National Holiday, Singapore
10 August	Independence Day, Ecuador
11 August	Independence Day, Chad (1960)
14 August	Independence Day, Pakistan (1947); Martyrdom of Maximilian Kolbe
15 August	Independence Day, India (1947); Independence Day, Korea

17 August	Independence Day, Gabon (1960) and Indonesia (1945)
24 August	Flag Day, Liberia
25 August	Independence Day, Uruguay (1825)
31 August	St Aidan; Independence Day, Trinidad & Tobago (1962); National Day, Malaysia
6 September	Independence Day, Swaziland
7 September	Independence Day, Brazil (1822)
8 September	National Day, Malta
9 September	National Holiday, Bulgaria
10 September	National Holiday, Bulgaria and Belize
14 September	Holy Cross Day
15 September	Independence Day, El Salvador (1841), Guatemala (1821) and Honduras (1821); Respect for the Aged Day in Japan
16 September	Independence Day, Papua New Guinea
18 September	Independence Day, Chile (1810)
20 September	Saints and Martyrs of Australia and the Pacific
21 September	Independence Day, Malta (1964)
22 September	Independence Day, Mali (1960)
23 September	National Day, Saudi Arabia
24 September	Independence Day, Guinea
26 September	Martyrs of North America
27 September	Independence Day, Mexico (1821)
30 September	Botswana Day (1966); 1st Commissioning of CMS Missionaries (1812)
1 October	National Day, Nigeria
2 October	National Days China (and 3rd); Guinea Independence Day (1958)
3 October	National Foundation Day, Korea
4 October	Independence Day, Lesotho (1966); St Francis of Assisi
8 October	National Poetry Day
9 October	Korean Alphabet Day; Independence Day, Uganda; National Day of Dignity, Peru
10 October	Fiji Day; Physical Education Day, Japan; National Day, Taiwan
12 October	Independence Day, Equatorial Guinea (1968); Republic Day, Sudan
13 October	Paulinus, Missionary Bishop
17 October	Mothers' Day, Malawi
18 October	Alaska Day
19 October	Henry Martin
20 October	Kenyatta Day, Kenya
24 October	United Nations Day; Independence Day, Zambia (1964)
26 October	National Day, Iran and Austria
28 October	National Day, Greece
29 October	James Hannington (1885); National Day, Turkey
1st full week in October	Children's Activity week (UK)
2nd week in October	Prisoners of Conscience week (Amnesty International)
3rd week in October	One World Week
3rd Friday in October	World Food Day
2nd Sunday in October	Racial Justice Sunday
1 November	All Saints Day; National Day, Algeria
3 November	Culture Day in Japan; National Day, Panama
7 November	Revolution Day in Bangladesh (1971)
8 November	Saints and Martyrs of England
9 November	National Day, Cambodia
10 November	Meeting of Stanley and Livingstone at Ujiji on the east shore of Lake Tanganika (1871)
11 November	St Martin of Tours
18 November	Independence Day, Morocco
20 November	International Day for the Rights of Children
22 November	National Day, Lebanon
23 November	Labour Thanksgiving Day, Japan
25 November	Independence Day, Surinam
26 November	Independence Day, Lebanon (1941)
28 November	Republic Day, Burundi (1966)
29 November	Day of Intercession and Thanksgiving for the missionary work of the church
30 November	St Andrew; CMS Day of Prayer
2nd full week in November	National Refugee Week
Last weekend in November	National Youth Sunday
3rd Sunday in November	Day of Prayer for the Persecuted Church
3rd week in November	Prisoners' Week
Final Thursday in November	Thanksgiving Day, USA
1 December	World AIDS Day; National Holiday, Central African Republic
3 December	Saints and Martyrs of Asia; Francis Xavier
5 December	National Day, Thailand
7 December	Independence Day, Ivory Coast Republic

8 December	Mothers' Day, Panama; Beach Day in Uruguay
9 December	Independence Day, Tanzania (1961)
10 December	Anniversary of the UN Declaration of Human Rights
12 December	Independence Day, Kenya (1963); Constitution Day (Thailand)
13 December	Republic Day, Malta
16 December	National Day, Bangladesh
18 December	National Day, Niger
25 December	Family Day, Angola
28 December	Massacre of the Innocents

– Appendix 3 –

Key questions

4-7 years (Foundation and Key Stage 1 / P1-3)

For Religious Education

- **AT1**: What different forms does Christianity take in another country outside the United Kingdom?
- **AT2**: What can we learn from the way Christians in another country worship God and love their neighbours?

For PSHE

- **AT1**: What difference does being a Christian make to a community in another part of the world?
- **AT2**: What can we learn for ourselves from how important Christianity is to believers in other parts of the world?

7-11 years (Key Stage 2 / P4-7)

For Religious Education

- **AT1**: What can we learn about what Christians believe—doctrine and practice—by exploring the worldwide Christian Church?
- **AT2**: What can we learn from the Christian faith as it is expressed in countries and cultures different from our own?

For PHSE and Global Citizenship

- **AT1**: How do Christians from the worldwide Church relate to their local communities and express their faith in practical action?
- **AT2**: What can Christians from around the world teach us about being citizens of the world?

Learning objectives

4-7 years (Foundation and Key Stage 1 / P1-3)

For Religious Education

- To discover some ways in which Christianity is differently expressed within another culture, and also what parts of Christianity are the same across cultures.

For PSHE

- To explore some ways in which Christians have made a positive impact on a community in a country outside the United Kingdom.

7-11 years (Key Stage 2 / P4-7)

For Religious Education

- To consider what Christians from other countries can teach us about Christian belief and practice and the difference it makes to their lives and communities.

For PHSE and Global Citizenship

- To explore the character of Christianity as a world faith and its contribution to global citizenship and human development.

Learning outcomes

4-7 years (Foundation and Key Stage 1 / P1-3)

For Religious Education

- That children will recognise that there are Christians in other countries who share basic beliefs about Jesus, even though they may express those beliefs in different ways.

For PSHE

- That children will have encountered at least one way in which Christians from another country are making a difference for good where they live, and also what the children might learn from it for themselves.

7-11 years (Key Stage 2 / P4-7)

For Religious Education

- That children will be able to recognise and understand different expressions of Christianity from around the world and compare and contrast them with the Christian Church in the United Kingdom.

For PHSE and Global Citizenship

- That children will be able to appreciate and celebrate difference better, both globally and within their own local community.

Learning experiences

4-7 years (Foundation and Key Stage 1 / P1-3)

- By means of an imaginative narrative about the migration of a swallow, children will encounter some stories of Christian believers in countries outside the United Kingdom.
- Using music, visuals and participative learning, children will explore how Christians in other parts of the world express their faith through baptism, Communion, worship, prayer and celebrations of special festivals.
- Through drama based on true-life stories, children will investigate the growth and spread of Christianity into a worldwide faith.
- Working with a few key stories, children will discover what the Bible says about the growth of the kingdom of God.

7-11 years (Key Stage 2 / P4-7)

- Through the narrative device of a story of bird migration, children will have the opportunity to encounter a variety of contrasting Christian communities across the world.
- Through ethical and reciprocal links with schools or churches in the majority world, children will be able to find out what being a Christian means for people in other countries.
- Using a range of source material, including information on the web, children will consider the contribution of Christians from countries outside the United Kingdom to issues of justice, inequality and the environment.
- Drawing on examples of differing global approaches to the expression of Christianity—including artwork, symbolism and ways of worship—children will be encouraged to draw their own conclusions about core Christian beliefs and practices.
- By engaging in debate and class discussions, children will be encouraged to think about what Christians in different parts of the world might give to and receive from each other in a worldwide family of faith.
- Working with passages from the Bible, children will explore what Christians believe about global rights and responsibilities.

– Appendix 4 –

Further resources

Prayers

African Prayers, Robert van de Weyer, O Books

A World of Prayer, Naomi Starkey, BRF

Prayers Encircling the World, SPCK

An African Prayer Book, Desmond Tutu, Hodder and Stoughton

Hallelujah for the Day: An African prayer book, Anthony J. Gittins, DLT

From Shore to Shore, SPCK/USPG

Poems and Prayers for a Better World, Su Box and Felicity Henderson, Lion

Morning, Noon and Night, John Carden, CMS

Another Day: Prayers of the human family, John Carden, Triangle

A Procession of Prayers, John Carden, Cassell

Stories and poems

The Oxford Treasury of World Stories, Michael Harrison and Christopher Stuart-Clark, OUP

Around the World in 80 Poems, James Berry, Macmillan

The Barefoot Book of Tropical Tales, Raouf Mama, Barefoot Books

Songs for Survival, Nikki Siegen-Smith, Barefoot Books

Stories from Native North America, Linda Raczek, Wayland

Lao Lao of Dragon Mountain, Margaret Bateson-Hill, Zero to Ten

Look Lively, Rest Easy, Helen East, A and C Black

Stories from West Africa, Robert Hall, Wayland

Stories from China, Saviour Pirotta, Wayland

Stories from the Amazon, Saviour Pirotta, Wayland

Stories from India, Vayu Naidu, Wayland

Stories from the Caribbean, Petronella Breinburg, Wayland

Too Much Talk: West African folk-tale, Angela Shelf-Medearin, Walker

South and North and East and West, Michael Rosen, Walker

Tales from the African Plains, Anna Gatti, Dutton

A Twist in the Tail, Mary Hoffman, Frances Lincoln

One Child, One Seed, Kathryn Cave, Frances Lincoln/Oxfam

Ebele's Favourite, Ifeoma Onyefulu, Frances Lincoln

Proverbs from Far and Near, Axel Scheffler, Ted Smart

When the World Began, Elizabeth Laird, OUP

The Lion Book of Wisdom Stories from Around the World, David Self, Lion

The Lion Storyteller Bedtime Book, Bob Hartman, Lion

The Lion Storyteller Christmas, Bob Hartman, Lion

The Lion Storyteller Book of Animal Tales, Bob Hartman, Lion

Bring the Rain to Kapiti Plains, Verna Aardema, Macmillan

The Colour of Home, Mary Hofman and Karin Littlewood, Frances Lincoln

Home Now, Lesley Beake and Karin Littlewood, Frances Lincoln

Almez and the Lion, Jane Kurtz, Puffin

A Fistful of Pearls and Other Tales from Iraq, Elizabeth Laird, Frances Lincoln

The Ogress and the Snake, Elizabeth Laird, Frances Lincoln

The World Came to My Place Today, Jo Readman and Ley Honor Roberts, Eden Project

Spirit of the Forest, Helen East, Eric Maddern and Alan Marks, Frances Lincoln

My Village, Danielle Wright, Frances Lincoln

Pictures, art and symbols

The Image of Christ, National Gallery

Christ for All People: Celebrating a world of Christian art, Ron O'Grady (ed.), WCC/Pace and the Asian Christian Art Association

A-cross the World, Martyn Payne and Betty Pedley, Barnabas

Picturing Jesus: Worldwide contemporary artists, Pack B, Christian Education

The Bible through Art, Margaret Cooling, National Gallery/Stapleford Project

Jesus through Art, Margaret Cooling, National Gallery/Stapleford Project

Jesus Mafa: Images from West Africa, www.jesusmafa.com

Anthology resources for worship

Born Among Us: Worldwide resources for Christmas, Methodist Church/USPG/Church of Ireland

The Christ We Share: Worldwide pictures of Jesus, Methodist Church/USPG/CMS/Church of Ireland

Touching the Pulse: Worship and our diverse world, Leslie Griffiths, Stainer and Bell

Gifts of Many Cultures, Maren Tirabassi and Kathy Eddy, United Church Press

A World of Blessing, Geoffrey Duncan, Canterbury Press

Shine On, Star of Bethlehem, Geoffrey Duncan, Canterbury Press and Christian Aid

Wisdom is Calling, Geoffrey Duncan, Canterbury Press

Timeless Prayers for Peace, Geoffrey Duncan, Canterbury Press

What a World, Geoffrey Duncan, Granary Press

The Christian Aid Book of Bread, Sarah Stancliffe, Christian Aid and Canterbury Press

What Does the Lord Require? Prayers and songs for worship, Francis Brienen (comp.), Canterbury Press and CWM

365 Ways to Make a Difference, Peter Greystone, Canterbury Press and Christian Aid

Out of the Toy Box, Renita Boyle and Heather Butler, Barnabas

Just Trade, Monica Philbrick, Kevin Mayhew

Sharing Ways and Wisdom, Barbara Butler, Kevin Mayhew

Windows on the World Church, Barbara Butler, Kevin Mayhew

Music resources

Sing through the Day: 80 songs for children worldwide, Plough Publishing

One is the Body, Wild Goose

Many and Great, Wild Goose

Sent by the Lord Am I, Wild Goose

Love and Anger, Wild Goose

There Is One among Us, Wild Goose

Freedom is coming: South African protest songs, Wild Goose

Journeys through Song, Christian Aid

Drawn to the Wonder, CWM

Songs, Games, Stories from around the World, Unicef

Many Voices, One Song (CD), WEC

In Every Corner Sing, published by RSCM, available from CMS

Organisations and websites

Anglican Communion: www.anglicancommunion.org

Council for World Mission: www.cwmission.org

Baptist Mission Society: www.bmsworldmission.org

Methodist Church (click on World Mission): www.methodist.org.uk

United Reformed Church: www.urc.org.uk/mission.html

Salvation Army: www.salvationarmy.org

Christian Aid: www.christianaid.org.uk

Oxfam: www.oxfam.org.uk

Tear Fund: www.tearfund.org

World Vision: www.worldvision.org.uk

CAFOD: www.cafod.org.uk

CMS: www.cms-uk.org

OMF: www.omf.org.uk

Wycliffe: www.wycliffe.org.uk

Unicef: www.unicef.org

Viva: www.viva.org

Smile International: www.smileinternational.org

Embrace the Middle East (formerly Bible*Lands*): www.embraceme.org

A useful website for crafts, stories, games and information from around the world: http://aroundtheworldin40weeks.com/about

Statistics

Atlas of World Christianity, Peter Brierley and Heather Wraight, OM Publishing/Christian Research

The Church is Bigger than You Think, Patrick Johnstone, Christian Focus/WEC International

Background information

A is for Africa, Ifeoma Oneyfulu, Frances Lincoln

B is for Bangladesh, Urmi Rahman, Frances Lincoln

B is for Brazil, Maria de Fatima Campos, Frances Lincoln

C is for China, Sungwan So, Frances Lincoln

I is for India, Prodeepta Das, Frances Lincoln

J is for Jamaica, Benjamin Zephaniah and Prodeepta Das, Frances Lincoln

K is for Korea, Hyechong Chung, Frances Lincoln

M is for Mexico, Flor de Maria Cordero, Frances Lincoln

P is for Pakistan, Shazia Razzak, Frances Lincoln

P is for Poland, Agnieszka Mrowczynska, Frances Lincoln

R is for Russia, Vladimir Kabakov and Prodeepta Das, Frances Lincoln

S is for South Africa, Beverley Naidoo and Prodeepta Das, Frances Lincoln

T is for Turkey, Nilufer Topaloglu Pyper and Prodeepta Das, Frances Lincoln

W is for World, Kathryn Cave, Frances Lincoln

One Day We Had to Run, Sybella Wilkes, Evans

If the World Were a Village, David Smith and Shelagh Armstrong, Black

'Don't Forget Us' series: for example, *I Come from... Romania*, Anita Ganeri, Watts

Traditions from Africa, Vivien Golding, Wayland

A Flavour of West Africa, Alison Brownlie, Wayland (part of a longer series)

A Taste of China, Roz Denny, Wayland (part of a longer series)

God's Everywhere People, Martyn Payne, CMS

Revolutionary Christians who Live the Gospel, Clare Richards, Kevin Mayhew

Papercrafts around the World, Phyllis and Noel Fiarotta, Stirling

'World Crafts' series by Meryl Doney, Watts (Masks, Games, Toys, Textiles, Musical Instruments, Festivals, Puppets, Jewellery)

A Life Like Mine: How children live around the world, Dorling Kindersley

Children of Britain Just Like Me, Barnabas and Anabel Kindersley, Unicef/Dorling Kindersley

Children Just Like Me, Barnabas and Anabel Kindersley, Dorling Kindersley

The Great World Tour, Kamini Khanduri, Usborne

Round the World Cookbook, Caroline Young, Usborne

For Every Child: The rights of the child in words and pictures, Caroline Castle, Red Fox/Unicef

How the World Works: An Oxfam guide, David Thorpe, Two-can/ Oxfam

Wake Up, World, Beatrice Hollyer, Frances Lincoln/ Oxfam

You Can Change the World, Jill Johnstone, OM Publishing

You Too Can Change the World, Daphne Spraggett, OM Publishing

Window on the World, Jill Johnstone and Daphne Spraggett, Paternoster/WEC

Helping Children to Care for God's People, Delia Halverson, Abingdon

Global Perspectives on Christianity, Janet King, RMEP/ Stapleford

A Calendar of Festivals, Cherry Gilchrist, Barefoot Books

The World Christian, Robin Thomson, Lynx

Divine Mosaic, Paul-Gordon Chandler, Triangle

Children in Crisis (Briefings), Glenn Myers, OM

Multi-Sensory World, Craig Borlase, SU

Index of activities

Glossary

Apartheid	A political policy designed to separate people on the grounds of race and colour; most notably the system that prevailed in South Africa during much of the 20th century.
Apostles	The title traditionally given to the first followers of Christ and other early Christian leaders after the death and resurrection of Jesus.
Baptise	To sprinkle with or immerse in water as part of a ceremony for those who are beginning the Christian journey of faith.
Catacombs	Underground tombs in Rome where many of the first Christians used to meet in secret.
Catholic	Someone who belongs to the branch of the Christian faith that acknowledges the Pope both as Christ's representative on earth and the supreme authority in matters of faith and doctrine.
Christen	Another word for 'baptise' (see above) but usually applied only to the baptism of a baby or young child.
Congregation	A group of Christian believers gathered for a service of worship.
Denominations	Groups of Christians who subscribe to an agreed set of interpretations about their shared Christian faith and who recognise one particular internal authority structure.
Disciples	The first followers of Jesus—traditionally the twelve who were specially called by him in the Gospel narratives. However, any Christians from any age can be described as disciples, which means 'learners' of the faith.
Doctrines	The key beliefs of a faith.
Eucharist	The central Christian service of worship, which involves the sacrament [see below] of bread and wine. It is also known as the Lord's Supper, the Mass, Communion and the Breaking of Bread.
Fast	To go without food for a period of time as a deliberate spiritual discipline—for example, in order to devote more time to prayer.
Genuflect	To bend the knee out of respect, usually before an altar or shrine; often accompanied by making the sign of the cross across one's upper body.
Godparents	Christian adults who commit themselves to pray for and support someone who is baptised.
Icons	Religious works of art, usually from the Orthodox Church [see below], that are produced according to a stylised, time-honoured pattern and depict scenes from the life of Jesus or stories of the saints. They are 'written' prayerfully and provide believers with a window into Christian truths, a stimulus to prayer and a way into the presence of God.
Incarnation	A term to describe what happened at Christmas when, Christians believe, God became a human being in the person of Jesus.
Jesse Tree	A model tree or part of a real tree, decorated during Advent (the four weeks before Christmas) with objects representing either biblical characters who were descended from Jesse, or other Old Testament symbols or heroes. The Old Testament prophets predicted that God's chosen king (or Messiah) would come from the family line of King David, whose father was Jesse. Christians therefore believe that Jesus was part of Jesse's family tree.
Martyrs	Traditionally, those Christians who, when faced with persecution, choose to be killed rather than deny their faith in God.

Mass Another name for the Eucharist [see above], used mainly within the Catholic tradition.

Minaret A tower on a mosque from which Muslim believers hear the call to prayer five times a day.

Monastic Anything that belongs to a monastery or its way of life. A monastery consists of a church and other related buildings where Christian monks worship and serve their local community.

Orthodox The branch of the Christian tradition that traces its roots back to the very first churches in the Middle East and whose worship is distinguished by colourful ritual and the use of icons [see above]. There are several groupings of Orthodox churches, including Russian, Coptic, Ethiopian and Syrian Orthodox.

Paschal A word used in relation to a Christian's pilgrimage through Lent to Easter (from a Greek word that means 'journey'). It is most often used as an adjective that alludes to the suffering and death of Jesus—hence 'the paschal mystery'.

Posada Spanish for 'inn'; used to describe the custom (which began in Mexico) of taking a Christmas crib from house to house during Advent to prepare people for Christmas.

Protestant Those Christian denominations [see above] that protested against the doctrines and practices of the Catholic Church in 16th-century Europe. They can broadly be described as Christians who make the Bible their ultimate authority in matters of Christian belief.

Relics Sacred objects, including the physical remains of the saints, which were believed in the Middle Ages to possess special powers. Many churches and cathedrals housed these relics in ornate shrines, which became a focus for worship and pilgrimage.

Resurrection The central tenet of Christian belief—namely, that Jesus Christ came back from the dead on the third day after his death on a cross.

Sacrament An element of several important services in Christian worship, in which ordinary objects, such as rings, oil, bread and wine, are used to symbolise some of the spiritual and mysterious truths of Christian belief.

Sect A group of people who separate themselves off from the traditional mainstream of a faith, usually involving an exclusive practice of a minority doctrine [see above] and devotion to a new breakaway leader.

By Martyn Payne with Betty Pedley

A-Cross the World

An exploration of 40 representations of the cross from the worldwide Christian Church

Around the world today, the cross is, arguably, the one universally recognised symbol of the Christian faith, but this unifying sign for diverse Christian communities has been much adapted, decorated and interpreted to convey particular stories that are dear to the community from which they come.

This book tells the stories behind 40 crosses from a wide diversity of cultures and Christian faith traditions and sets out to promote discussion and debate on why this single, historical event continues to exercise such an influence worldwide.

Section One contains stories, information, Bible links, wondering questions and suggested activities on the 40 crosses, as well as photocopiable illustrations of each cross. The material for this section was originally produced in-house by the Church Mission Society.

Section Two contains a wealth of extension material ideal for use in the classroom at Key Stage 1 and 2, in collective worship and in church-based activities, including icebreakers, games, prayers and poems, crafts and session outlines for special activity days, assemblies, holiday clubs and all-age worship.

Includes photocopy permission.

ISBN 978 0 85746 074 5   £15.99
Available from your local Christian bookshop or direct from BRF: please visit www.barnabasinschools.org.uk.

The Big Story

36 session outlines and reflective Bible stories exploring six big themes of God's love

The Big Story contains a treasure bank of creative, visual storytelling sessions designed to unpack six big Bible themes. The approach connects up the whole story of the Bible and attempts to give an overview of God's purposes by seeing the Bible not as a collection of unrelated events but as an amazing and ordered revelation of God's love.

Each of the 36 sessions contains a wealth of thought-provoking activities and reflective ideas to accompany the storytelling. The material includes an initial overview in the form of a visual timeline of Bible history, designed to help children and their leaders gain the bigger perspective. The six themes are then each introduced by a reflective story that acts as an anchor for a further six individual stories.

The big themes explore:

- Enemies and friends: God's longing for friendship with and between all people.
- Dark and light: the first gift of creation and abiding reality of re-creation.
- Famine and feast: the rhythm of abundance and shortage.
- Death and life: God's heart for bringing life out of places of destruction.
- Depths and heights: journeying with God from despair to joy.
- Hide and seek: experiencing the immediate presence and apparent absence of God.

The material can be used in a variety of ways:

- As a stand-alone resource to begin thinking about special times of year.
- To give an overview before picking out two or three of the individual stories.
- As a three-term programme with one big theme being explored in each half-term period.

ISBN 978 1 84101 812 6 £10.99
Available from your local Christian bookshop or direct from BRF: please visit www.barnabasinschools.org.uk.

Bethlehem Carols Unpacked

Creative ideas for Christmas carol services

Lucy Moore and Martyn Payne

This book uses eleven well-known carols that appear in Embrace the Middle East's *Bethlehem Carol Sheet* to explore many different aspects of the Christmas message. It includes ideas to create an imaginative carol service, designed to draw in those attending and to provide a truly memorable act of worship.

Linked to the work of Embrace the Middle East's partners, the resource is packed with interesting facts about the carols, extended Bible references and a wealth of all-age, practical, theme-based ideas for creative storytelling, poetry, prayers, drama and worship. The book is structured using a flexible pick-and-mix formula, designed to assist people at all levels of experience with the planning of a carol service. A special section for those under the age of five is also included, making the material suitable for toddler groups, preschool playgroups and pram services.

- Away in a manger
- Once in royal David's city
- God rest you merry, gentlemen
- Silent night
- Good King Wenceslas
- The first Nowell
- Hark! the herald-angels sing
- We three kings
- O come, all ye faithful
- While shepherds watched
- O little town of Bethlehem

The material has been co-written by the Barnabas Children's Ministry team and Embrace the Middle East to highlight the charity's work, which is celebrated by many who use the *Bethlehem Carol Sheet*. For further information about Embrace the Middle East, please visit www.embraceme.org.

Drama out of a Crisis

20 challenging, fun and inspirational sketches about poverty and justice

Peter Shaw

Drama out of a Crisis comprises 20 short, easy-to-perform sketches providing a fresh perspective on some of the world's most pressing issues.

Designed to engage and explore the issues without being didactic or guilt-inducing, the sketches are organised under specific themes and accompanied by real-life background information, a biblical context and suggestions for follow-up.

Themes include:

- Prayer and poverty
- Ending violence against women
- Food security
- Natural disasters
- Malaria
- Climate change
- Living with HIV
- Trade justice
- Global sanitation crisis
- Fair trade
- Water crisis
- Governance and corruption
- Education and poverty
- Speaking out
- Children at risk
- Church mobilisation
- Maternal health
- Church & community mobilisation
- The Bible and poverty

ISBN 978 0 85746 005 9 £7.99
Available from your local Christian bookshop or direct from BRF: please visit www.barnabasinschools.org.uk.

Poetry Emotion

50 original poems to spark an imaginative approach to topical values

Stewart Henderson

Poetry Emotion contains a treasure trove of original poems to stimulate a child's observation and deep thinking; to affirm individuality and a sense of belonging; to express a myriad of feelings; and to develop meaningful skills for living.

The 50 poems are organised under 15 topic-based chapters, providing an ideal vehicle to address social and emotional values with 7–11s. They can be used with great effect in Collective Worship, and are readily related to English, PSHCE and RE in the classroom.

The poems in each section are offered with introductory suggestions for ways in which the topics can be unpacked. Topics include:

- Whose world?
- Who am I?
- Who is my neighbour?
- What's so special about the Bible?
- It's not fair!
- Getting on and falling out
- Going for goals
- New beginnings
- Saying no to bullying
- Good to be me
- Changes
- Self-awareness
- Managing feelings
- Motivation
- Social skills

ISBN 978 1 84101 893 5 £6.99
Available from your local Christian bookshop or direct from BRF: please visit www.barnabasinschools.org.uk.

Story Assemblies of 24 Saints

24 off-the-peg assembly plans for the school year

Heather Butler

Story Assemblies of 24 Saints features a wealth of saints' days spread across the school year from September to July, making it an ideal ongoing resource and enabling teachers to opt in at any time.

The material contains 24 complete assembly plans ready for teachers to pick off the shelf and deliver as a whole-school, year-group or classroom assembly.

Each outline comprises a creative mix of elements, designed to highlight a special feature about the saint and help children use their imaginations to ground the story. Topical links are included to encourage children to think about what the message of the story might mean to their own lives today.

ISBN 978 1 84101 703 7   £7.99
Available from your local Christian bookshop or direct from BRF: please visit www.barnabasinschools.org.uk.

Story Assemblies for the School Year

36 assemblies with five-minute stories, teacher's notes and RE follow-up

Edward J. Carter

This book is full of memorable stories, designed to engage and delight pupils at primary level. The stories are essentially parables about God and the events in the Bible, creatively told to help children understand the big story of God's love for the world. Pupils are invited to imagine themselves as part of the story and also encouraged to think about their own values and behaviour, not by learning the right answers to give, but by making a leap of imagination and identifying themselves with the characters in the stories.

There are six themes in total, each with its own easy-to-make storytelling prop. The stories within each theme are divided into six weekly episodes, covering a wide range of contemporary values and topics. Together the stories cover the whole school year, with a key theme and a story in six parts for each half-term period. At the end of each half-term there is a special assembly to mark that part of the school year: harvest, Christmas, Christingle or Pancake Day, Holy Week or Easter, Pentecost, and a leavers' farewell.

As well as being ideal for collective worship, there are practical follow-up ideas to help children connect with the stories in the classroom.

The six themes cover:

- God's creation
- The message of the Old Testament prophets
- Stories about Christian values
- The story of Holy Week and Easter
- Jesus' resurrection and ascension
- The journeys of the apostle Paul

Story Assemblies for the School Year Volume 2

36 assemblies with five-minute stories, teacher's notes and RE follow-up

Edward J. Carter

A second year's worth of assembly material for those who enjoyed *Story Assemblies for the School Year*.

Again, there are six themes in total, each with its own easy-to-make storytelling prop. The stories within each theme are divided into six weekly episodes, covering a wide range of contemporary values and topics. Together the stories cover the whole school year, with a key theme and a story in six parts for each half-term period. At the end of each half-term there is a special assembly to mark that part of the school year: harvest, Christmas, Lent, Easter, Pentecost, and a leavers' farewell.

As well as being ideal for collective worship, there are practical follow-up ideas to help children connect with the stories in the classroom.

The six themes cover:

- The exodus
- The promised land
- The disciples of Jesus
- The judgment parables
- The first Christians
- Paul's letters

ISBN 978 0 85746 059 2 £8.99
Available from your local Christian bookshop or direct from BRF: please visit www.barnabasinschools.org.uk.

Enjoyed this book?

Write a review—we'd love to hear what you think. Email: reviews@brf.org.uk

Keep up to date—receive details of our new books as they happen. Sign up for email news and select your interest groups at: www.brfonline.org.uk/findoutmore/

Follow us on Twitter @brfonline

By post—to receive new title information by post (UK only), complete the form below and post to: BRF Mailing Lists, 15 The Chambers, Vineyard, Abingdon, Oxfordshire, OX14 3FE

Your Details

Name ______________________________

Address ______________________________

____

Town/City ____________________ Post Code ____________

Email ______________________________

Your Interest Groups (*Please tick as appropriate)

- ☐ Advent/Lent
- ☐ Bible Reading & Study
- ☐ Children's Books
- ☐ Discipleship
- ☐ Leadership
- ☐ Messy Church
- ☐ Pastoral
- ☐ Prayer & Spirituality
- ☐ Resources for Children's Church
- ☐ Resources for Schools

Support your local bookshop

Ask about their new title information schemes.